KAP

Making a Start on Child Study

LESLEY WEBB

OXFORD · BASIL BLACKWELL

0 631 16480 4

By the same author:

Modern Practice in the Infant School
Purpose and Practice in Nursery Education

Printed in Great Britain by
Billing & Sons Limited
Guildford, London, Oxford and Worcester

Contents

Introduction

This book is intended for anyone wishing to make a serious study of children, whether as student teacher or nursery assistant, child-care worker, playgroup organizer or concerned parent. Anyone undertaking a course of training in connexion with caring for or teaching children, as well as teachers or others on advanced or conversion courses, is usually expected to 'make a child-study'—an exercise as important in the field of child nurture and education as is the study of anatomy to a doctor. Yet child-study is not always as well done as it might be by the novice, and may even be regarded by some as a waste of time if the resultant record is vague, generalized and sentimental. Many tutors have reservations about their own instructions to students, and almost all those whom I have met have been interested in refinement and revision of their own methods.

There is also doubt about whether the same guidance in studying children's everyday behaviour is appropriate to students as different in age and background as a girl of seventeen beginning an NNEB course and a mature student, with children of her own, training to teach. My view is that the nature of the task and the behaviour of children does not change with the age or experience of the observer, so it is unnecessary and somewhat patronizing to change methods of child-study according to the type of course and age of the student. At no point in this book, therefore, have I suggested methods or approaches more or less suitable for NNEB, playgroup or teacher-education courses. At the level of competent child-study all students are on an equal footing.

I have considered one basic technique (called *specimen description*) at length, and two others (*time-sampling* and *event-sampling*) in enough detail to make their use possible to the novice. All are observational techniques and require no specialized equipment, laboratory or psychological training for their proper use. Yet they are academically and scientifically respectable means of gathering information, and have a long history of use in many disciplines:

> Direct observation has been a methodological mainstay in many other sciences. It has stood as the basic method of astronomy and the earth sciences, of the natural history disciplines in biology, and of anthropology and sociology. Its contributions may not have been revolutionary so often as procedures that manipulate events; and yet they have been substantial over the long run of progress in science.[1]

'Studying child behaviour while leaving it alone', as the author of the above passage writes, is a fascinating, exacting and skilled task. Yet it can be mastered by anyone who has a genuine interest in children, reasonable patience and a clear mind. It yields information so valuable that the task is well worth the effort at mastery.

I claim no originality in this short guide. I have put between two covers and in short space much that already exists in the heads and notes of tutors and in larger American works not always easily available to students. I have used the approaches suggested in this guide with all kinds of students, ranging from seventeen to fifty, and on courses leading to widely different kinds of award. The results for those students have been satisfactory enough to suggest that others might find this kind of guidance useful while still in the novice stage—and a handy check-list once they become experienced.

Of course there are methods of child-study used by psychologists and paediatricians of which all who work with children should be aware—and of which they should have modest understanding, at least. Such methods as standardized tests, projective techniques and rating scales, laboratory-experimental methods and psychiatric interview have produced an enormous body of invaluable information on childhood, to which teachers and others are greatly indebted. But with the exception of some standardized tests especially intended for use by teachers they are highly specialized and best left to those trained in their use. The best and most proper 'tool' for the specialisms of teaching and child-care is accurate and intelligent observation. It is with this, and not with the methods of other specialists or with the complexities of statistical analysis of data, that this book is concerned.

[1] H. F. Wright, 'Observational Child Study' in *Handbook of Research Methods in Child Development*, Mussen (Ed.) Wiley, N.Y., 1960.

1. Justifications for Child Study

i

It is an interesting and enlightening exercise to ask various members of a family what a child of, perhaps, five or six was like as a baby or a two year old. One parent may say that he was a good baby; the other that he walked early and had to be watched every minute. One grandmother may tell you that he was spoiled and wilful; the other that he was as good as gold, and just like her son; while a grandfather may recall the child's independence and good sense at an early age. An older sister may remember nothing like this, but bring to mind his doings in nursery school with surprising clarity. There will be little family arguments about when such-and-such behaviour took place. What will be plain is that even people close to a child remember different things about him, telescope events, and even get two children of the family confused as they tell, in after years, anecdotes of 'when the children were small'. Just as a family has its own memories and even myths of childhood, based on fact but distorted by time and preference, so has a society. Children are expected to behave in a certain way at a certain age, to enjoy certain foods and dislike others, to play certain games, and treat adults in a particular manner. It is as though there were an 'ideal childhood' in the minds of parents—and, now, in the minds of advertisers, television producers and magazine photographers—to which children ought at least to approximate. Of course they never do, even

4

when out of imitative play, politeness or sheer boredom they threaten to become like the awful stereotypes some parents and most advertisers hold up as models.

What a child is really like, what he can do, what he enjoys doing, what he fears, and at which ages, for how long and in what manner, are matters of crucial concern to parents, teachers and others with responsibility for the day-to-day care of children. To believe that some 'norm' of behaviour is to be achieved by every child, or that children of a certain age 'ought' to be able to ride a tricycle, or read, or pay attention, or some such, is to deny individuality and subscribe to a myth. It is true that there are normal limits of growth and development outside which very few children fall. For example, we do not expect babies to be born with teeth (although a very few are), and we do expect them to be walking by the middle of the second year of life (although a few, rather heavier than average, may not be and still be quite normal). We should be astonished by a year-old child who could talk fluently with us; and equally astonished, even perturbed, by a four year old who could not. The point is that some of our expectations about what children 'ought' to be like and able to do are quite justifiable. What it is important to remember is how wide are the normal limits of development and how different are the ways and speeds in which individual children, even in the same family, go through the normal stages. We are not justified in assuming that what 'everybody says' about what children ought to be able to do at certain ages is necessarily true. It may be. But only by looking carefully for ourselves can we be reasonably sure. Similarly, the advice, 'norms' and commentary of the reputable textbooks may be a great help to us in understanding children—but believing 'what the book says' (instead of looking for ourselves and then going back to the book, which is the wise thing to do) can lead us into having some unrealistic expectations. Even the few children well known to a student of child behaviour must not be taken as 'typical' of whole age-groups. Children from different social and racial backgrounds, even children in different parts of the British Isles, may vary in many ways, even though of the

5

same ages, from children in a student's own family or classroom. There will be some truth in some generally held beliefs; there will be some marked similarities between children of the same age; but there will be crucial exceptions and many highly individual versions of 'being a baby' or of 'four year oldness'. We should strive to become aware of such exceptions and differences, in fairness to the children we are dealing with.

By looking at a child with no preconceived ideas of what he ought to be like; with as little reference in our minds as possible to what his mother, grandmother or teacher believes him to be like (it will be appropriate, later, to add their insights to our own); by looking at him, in fact, as though he were a new member of a new species of which we know nothing—we may get an idea of what he may really be like. It is very easy for any of us, in looking at anything, to see what we expect to see, what the rest of the world suggests to us is there, or what the book says will be there. Such unconscious attempts to fit our own experience into existing 'patterns' is natural and common enough—but that is how stereotypes are formed and false expectations developed. Good child-study, depending as it does on close observation of on-going behaviour, highly detailed recording as the behaviour proceeds, exact timing of the record, and subsequent careful analysis of the information, tends to explode the more absurd, unjust and unreasonable old wives' tales, the stereotypes and the unrealistic expectations of children some people express. If it did no more than this it would be worth mastering—but, of course, good child-study, as a technique, has other additional justifications.

ii

Because each human being is a unique organism—as is each individual of any species—we can never claim to know all there is to know about human behaviour. Since the beginning of this century there has been an explosion of knowledge about human development. The many branches of psychology and,

6

more recently, of sociology have produced tens of thousands of research papers, textbooks and techniques dealing with every human characteristic, with particular emphasis on the identification and measurement of individual differences. In the face of this massive output of expert theorizing, reporting and methodology the novice might be forgiven for thinking that there was nothing she could learn that has not already been reported somewhere, and in a form more skilled than any she could emulate. This is only true in a limited manner, in that almost certainly somebody, somewhere, has studied at depth the aspect of child behaviour the novice is interested in —a baby's response to his mother, a two year old's manipulative skills, a three year old's social behaviour, the language of a four year old, for example. But what no experienced teacher, psychologist or doctor can have done is to know, in intimate detail, the responses of the particular child or children, the student is playing with, caring for and teaching. These are unique, however akin to the responses of other children of like age, and have never been made in exactly this way by any child in the world before. The student's findings should, if the job is sensibly done, find near-parallels in the work of greater investigators—but the detail is her own, and in a real sense her observations are unique.

Much of the sound knowledge in the literature, gathered over the years by hundreds of investigators, may help the novice (and any of us) to select principles of approach to a certain problem of behaviour, teaching or learning—but it cannot tell her exactly what to do with the real child who is in a real relationship with her, on a particular day in a particular family, nursery group or school. What that child needs most, at that moment in his life, what are his special skills, fears, fads and loves—those the observer alone, if sensitive and caring enough, can go some way to finding out. After many such close observations of individuals the textbooks become more meaningful, in any case, and this is another most valuable use of child-study. The student who has herself learned to study children understands more and more as she reads what other investigators are saying. The children of the printed page 'come alive' to her as she recognizes bits and pieces of behaviour and certain characteristics as very similar to some she has observed in children she knows. Reading becomes an extension of personal experience, not a task of memorizing, when one has shared, in however modest a manner, the writer's field of investigation.

iii

Studying children well has another advantage beyond those of mastering a valuable technique and coming more easily to terms with the textbooks. It gives confidence to the teacher or other person who has the care of children when facing the questions asked by parents, doctor or nurse. It gives confidence to parents, asking questions of themselves. After a century of increasing 'expertise' in child-rearing, welfare and education, offered to them by doctors, health visitors and teachers, many young (and some not-so-young) mothers tend to lose confidence in their own powers of judgement about what they ought to do with their children. With the best of intentions, 'experts' from the clinic, the social services and the school have largely taken over from parents much that was once in their gift and their choice. It is hardly surprising that, having been told what to do in almost every aspect of child-care (and often in the most brisk and confident manner), some mothers feel themselves ignorant and inexpert, not competent to decide whether some behaviour is 'normal' or not, and that some become weakly dependent on anyone they view as 'expert' for advice in the most simple matters. To feel that the doctor, the nurse or the teacher should be consulted about such matters as what time a child should go to bed, how much he should eat, whether he should play at this or that, or whether he should be taught to read at the age of three is to abdicate responsibility—but it is probably the 'experts' themselves who have, if unintentionally, robbed young parents (and young people generally) of the ordinary self-confidence such everyday decisions demand of us.

One of the responsibilities of those who will work professionally with young children is to give back to parents some sense of confidence in themselves as parents, and to work with them rather than tell them what to do in matters of child-rearing or teaching. This is a complex and far from easy task for the young teacher or child-care worker. One of the ways in which she herself may find confidence is by studying individual children so well that she has real and quite individual comment to pass on to a worried or over-dependent mother. If the teacher or nurse has looked carefully at a child she may be the better able to pass on to the mother not only valuable information about that particular child (instead of stereotyped advice or comforting platitudes) but also insights and even some of the techniques needed for the mother to study her own child, and make her own judgements.

Not only does sound child-study, and careful recording of it, give the teacher or other responsible person something of real value to pass on to the child's parents, it is an invaluable means by which the observer can serve the school doctor or psychologist who asks for full information to help in making medical or guidance decisions. It is a sad reflection that the lack of close, controlled child-study, well recorded and analysed, may have been one of the omissions which led to the death of a seven year old (1973)—for good observations are good evidence, and evidence in the case referred to seemed miserably inexact and equivocal, as well as non-available to some concerned parties. In far less tragic circumstances than these, however, the well-made and well-presented child-study could save experts in other fields a great deal of time and prevent considerable misunderstanding. It is an expertise well worth developing if only for this purpose.

iv

Finally, one of the justifications for making observations of children in an orderly and exact manner is that such observations help teachers and others to set realistic goals for themselves and the children. At the beginning of this chapter one of the justifications given was the removal from our minds of stereotype, myth and unrealistic expectation about children's behaviour and learning. A good child-study gives us more than a clear picture of what a child is really like—it suggests clues to what he might be able to do, enjoy doing and not be ready to do in the near future. It gives guidance as to his needs for growth and learning, which enables us to 'meet him' at the point of growth, or gives us confidence 'to wait' and not to hurry him. It is not suggested that the busy teacher or nursery assistant in a nursery or infant class has time to make a close, observational study of every child, in order to produce an individual programme for each. This is patently impossible, and probably quite unnecessary. What is possible to mothers of younger children at home, however, is an occasional close look at the child, in the way shown later in this book.

In nursery and school groups it is possible to do an occasional study of a child who is a little unusual, of a perfectly ordinary child (in order to keep realistic standards and expectations), and of one or two children a term in different age-groups to ensure that activities are really helping progression. It is a fact that even an occasional close observation of one or two children is surprisingly helpful in sharpening awareness of all the others. The seeing eye can be trained, as can most senses, and the more we train ourselves to observe the more we see even when we are not actually making a child-study. Noticing what they really do, how, when and in what order, becomes a habit with the good teacher. Like all habits it can be encouraged by letting the novice practise it frequently. Once established, the ability to look without prejudice, to note detail, to assess a child's pace, needs and strengths makes for realistic goal-setting and consequent success and satisfaction for child and teacher alike.

Summary

Making good child-studies helps us to look objectively at children, and to reject old wives' tales, stereotypes, myths and common but unreasonable expectations about what children 'ought' to be like.

Every study based on sound observations is a unique contribution to knowledge and a means by which the writings of other (and more experienced) investigators can be more readily appreciated and understood.

Good, first-hand observations of children give the teacher or other responsible person relevant and valuable information to pass on to mothers who may be uncertain of their own judgement about their young children—information not only about the child, but about how he may be observed by the mother herself, if less formally than by the teacher. Well-recorded and analysed observations can be crucial information to pass on to other (legitimately concerned) persons, such as school doctor, health visitor, psychologist or social worker.

The setting of realistic goals for teachers and children, and the assessment of activities appropriate to individual children and particular age-groups, is served by making even a few thorough studies. Making observational child-studies of only a few children helps to develop the 'seeing eye' and the habit of constant assessment of children's real needs for growth and learning.

Note: The reader is probably asking, by this time. *What is a 'good' child study?* The rest of this book will, it is hoped, make the answer plain—but this chapter has intimated that to be 'good' a study will be, first:

    of on-going behaviour
    in as minute detail as possible
    without interpretation or opinion as it is recorded
    without manipulation of the situation
    without omission of 'disapproved' behaviour
    for an exactly recorded block of time

Secondly, the data thus recorded will be analysed to discover patterns (if any), similarities with behaviour recorded in textbooks, anomalies and idiosyncrasies—and the analysis presented in some simple table or graph.

Thirdly, there will be an essay-type summary of 'the whole child', or a written, short discussion of a particular part of his/her behaviour, or both.

Fourthly, the whole work will be neatly filed together, and a bibliography added.

the age of eighteen months or two years, and will have to 'take what offers' from the married sisters of fellow-students, mothers met during visits to nurseries and schools, or even from someone met in the launderette, whose baby she admired. This is all to the good, as such choices tend to cut out undue personal bias. The novice need not fear that any baby will be 'dull', or inactive, or not what she needs to study. (The sad exception to this may be a baby with more or less severe mental or physical handicap. It is not recommended that the novice, even with a limited choice available, selects such a child as a subject for her first three or four studies.)

The day nurseries are the exception to the general finding that babies are not usually gathered together in groups. Such places do provide a reasonably wide choice of babies to study —but the choice is not really random. Every baby and young child in a day nursery is likely to be there because there is a family problem. These problems will range from the temporary one of having mother away in hospital having another baby with no relatives to look after the older one, through having no father at home for reasons ranging from death, desertion or divorce to mother being unmarried or father in prison or mental hospital. Much valuable under-standing of children may be gained from visits to or work in a day nursery, and observation of the children there—but it must be remembered that such children almost always have deviant backgrounds (which is not to say that they are not loved and cared-for very well by a lone parent—they often are), and it is always wise to start learning about children by looking at those who enjoy what our society regards as a 'normal' family set-up. This is, simply, a family which consists of both parents, neither of whom is markedly deviant, living under the same roof. The presence of older brothers and sisters is, of course, normal in all but the most wealthy households (from which small boys of seven may be sent away to school, thus robbing younger siblings of big brothers around the place, and small boys of helping to bring up smaller ones). Normal, also, although less common than it was, is the presence of a grandmother or grandfather; the reasonably near

14

presence of relatives; the occasional presence in kitchen or living-rooms of friendly neighbours. Such a background is still the norm in most places. As a beginning it is only sensible to study a baby whose family is, in general terms, if not in detail, of this kind. After some experience of child-study the less fortunately placed child can be studied more realistically, and is less likely to be taken as 'typical'.

With these reservations and exceptions in mind (and tutorial advice should always be available if a student is not sure whether her choice of a baby to study is a suitable one), random choice can be made, and even the novice knows that she has started as a good observer should—with no bias. There are ways of behaving in someone else's home which are conducive to getting co-operative and friendly response from parents and children alike—and there are approaches which, however well-meant, tend to antagonize or embarrass families. Much more will be said about how to proceed in the next chapter. For the present it is enough to say that, having chosen a baby to study, the student is in a position of privilege. She has no 'rights' in the matter of visiting the baby's home, questioning the mother, or making notes. Membership of a college or of a course confers no right of entry whatsoever into people's homes—in which respect the student is subject only to the same restrictions as health visitor, doctor, or even police. Mothers usually like to have their babies made the subject of a study; but they do not have to offer that opportunity, and students should take careful note of subsequent advice in this book in order that future students continue to be offered the privilege of studying babies and young children in their own homes.

ii

Children of three and over, from 'normal' families (as in the definition given above), are gathered together in playgroups, nursery schools and classes, and in Infants' schools. The question of random choice would therefore appear simpler

15

than with babies. In fact, it is not. There is a wider choice, true—perhaps twenty young children in one group, up to eighty in a big nursery school, perhaps as many as forty in the reception and post-reception classes of an Infants' school. Yet with so many children of from three years to five from which to choose the danger of personal preference or teacher-direction to an 'interesting' child increases.

How does one select a child truly at random from among a group? Several methods are possible. When working in playgroup, nursery or Infants' school it is possible to look at the register of names and pick simply the fifth, tenth or n-th name from the list—with no previous inquiry about any child. A student could also decide, in advance, to study the first child who came in the door, or who crossed a certain point on the floor at a given time. Any of these devices prevents the possibility of unconscious bias in selection, as well as that well-meant direction by a more experienced person already mentioned.

If care is not taken to make the choice from a group random it will be found that any one of us tends to select the same kind of child every time. Normal preferences for this or that sex, this or that colouring, this or that behavioural characteristic, or temperament are deeply woven into our minds, well below everyday consciousness, from our own earliest childhood. It is part of being adult not to let such normal but unconscious preferences dictate our professional behaviour. Of course every student will have a preference for some kinds of appearance or temperament above others—little dark boys, or little fair girls, or children with freckles, or the smallest ones, or the sturdiest ones, or the ones with a handicap, and so on—but by making random choices of children to study she will find that every child is interesting, and will 'notice' not only those who appealed to the unconscious but many others as well. Random selection of a sample for study is one of the first principles adopted by research workers in every field from psychological medicine to consumer research, and in all other sciences as well. It makes for a 'fair picture'. The novice might as well, in the very simple and inevitably

16

unsophisticated ways suggested here, start her work by being as objective as it is possible to be in what are called 'the human sciences'.

There might be exceptions to the general rule of random selection for the student in some nursery groups and schools. It is possible that having selected the *n*-th name from the register, or decided to study the first child who comes in the door, that child will turn out to be the one immigrant, or mentally handicapped, or emotionally disturbed child in the whole group! It is then only sensible to start the selection process again. As indicated above, in discussion of handicapped babies and those at day nurseries, it is not wise to start one's practice of child-study with a deviant child, no matter how attractive or interesting he is, and no matter how a personal interest in a particular kind of handicap inclines the novice to that study. It is more helpful, at the beginning, to get a 'feel' for so-called ordinary children—each one of whom is different enough, in all conscience, from every other child to add something 'special' to every study. If a student finds herself in a group particularly biased towards handicapped children—and some nursery schools are now too loaded with what are called special cases—it may be sensible to write a list of all the ordinary children first, and then select a name at random from that list, rather than from the register. Only after several studies of children not markedly different from the average have been made is it fruitful, perhaps, to study a child with a noticeable problem. Even then, it is only common sense that the novice consult her tutor about making such a study.

Whether the student goes into a day nursery, school or PPA group, she is likely to have a choice of age-groups, if only between birth and three, three and five, or five and eight. It is advisable, in any case, to have made a study of several children under the age of two before moving on to study of older children. It is then advisable to study the less self-conscious threes and fours before taking a notebook to the more 'noticing' fives and sixes. To study older children than this really is beyond the scope of most novices, and it is the intention of

17

this book to suggest ways of 'making a start' rather than of going on to greater expertise. In any case, children above the age of seven or so are all too often sitting down doing individual work, or listening to the teacher, or playing organized games, or (at best) playing their own very active games out of doors. None of these situations is particularly helpful to the beginner. It is, therefore, with the age-groups from the first to seventh years of life with which this book is concerned, and with whom observational techniques are most likely to be useful.

In looking at a nursery school group of children the student would be well advised not to decide from the start that she prefers three years olds to fours, or under-threes to any of the rest. Each of these ages has great, and distinctive, charm. It is foolish to attempt to 'specialise' at the novice stage. The same holds for work in an Infants' school. Some student-teachers have been known to finish their training determined that they are not only going to teach six year olds (or 'top Infants', or 'reception', as the case may be)—but actually do not like, or do not know how to teach any others! The foolishness of this attitude may owe something to the college policy, but it probably owes more to the bias of the student herself; a bias that sensible selection of child-studies might have eliminated. The facts of adult life and employment are that no one can be that much of a specialist. A teacher who claims that she can only teach one age-group, or an NNEB certificated girl who 'doesn't want to know' about any children but two year olds, is a pretty poor employment prospect for any authority. Such limited folk are few, no doubt. But the unconscious preferences mentioned earlier can operate in respect of age-preferences, as well as appearance and temperament—and they really must be overcome early in any career.

There is no need to work at child-studies in chronological order. Given a choice of children between two and five, or four and seven, the novice may, by all means, start by studying a child in an age-group for which she has a particularly 'soft spot'. But what she ought to have produced, after a period of time varying from a term to the whole of her course, is a set of studies of children from the first year of life to the fifth, sixth or seventh (according to whether she is going to be a mainly nursery specialist, or work in an Infants' school or children's home where older children will be accommodated). There is no need for a set in each age-group, but, ideally, there ought to be more than one in each of the main age-groups with which her career is likely to be spent. Certainly, as she selects children to study throughout her course, she should have in mind that her final 'set' of well-made studies should not be of children in a narrow age-band. No matter in which kind of institution she is going to work, and no matter in what capacity, anyone working with children should have at least some understanding not only of the entire age-range she deals with every day but of the age-groups immediately 'below' and immediately 'above' it.

Summary

It is essential that choice of a subject for child-study be as random as possible, to reduce the possibility of personal bias or preference affecting choice.

Random choice may be inevitable when studying babies, or children below even nursery age, as these children are likely to be at home with their mothers, and not gathered into groups (as in school) where the choice is wider for the student. She may have to 'take what offers'—and this is likely to ensure that the choice was free of personal bias.

Babies and very young children in day nurseries are not recommended for child-study by the novice, as they are (inevitably) in the day nursery because there is a family difficulty of some kind. They cannot, therefore, be regarded as having a normal social background. It is advisable to leave study of such children until experience has been gained with more fortunate children, in their own homes, and interacting with members of their own families.

A baby with mental or physical handicap is also not a good subject for study by the novice.

It is important to remember that nobody has a right of entry to anyone's home—and students should be most courteous and tactful in making studies of babies and children at home.

Random choice in school is not as simple as it might seem. There are simple ways of ensuring that one does make a random choice, however, and one of these should always be employed.

In studying children at school, day nursery, playgroup or other place where a choice of age-groups is available, a student should aim to make a study of children in several age-groups—and not let herself be persuaded by unconscious preference (or anything else) to become a 'one age-group specialist'. This is not helpful to future employers, or to anyone contemplating a responsible career in teaching or child-care.

At the end of her course a student should have a set of studies covering children in the whole age-range she is likely to deal with plus at least one study of a child immediately 'below' and one immediately 'above' that range.

3. Establishing Contact with Parents, Nurseries and Schools

i

It has already been suggested (Chapter 2, above) that the best way to start on child-study is with a baby—and by 'baby', for the purposes of this book, is meant a child of from birth to something like eighteen months of age. Beyond this stage, almost every child has attained the skill of getting about on his own, has acquired a sort of vocal skill which, if not yet quite recognizable as fluent language, is remarkably efficient (over many situations he meets, if not all) as a means of communication. A baby is an easier 'subject' for the novice because he is rather more static than an older child—although this is by no means the same as saying that less is happening as he plays, is bathed, interacts with people, and so on. It is to say, however, that he keeps more or less in one place, unless carried somewhere else, and the inexpert observer is not faced with the problem of recording a child who is cruising out of sight. Studying a child of two or three can resemble being at the Queen of Hearts' croquet ground—no sooner does the observer, like Alice, succeed in getting her flamingo and hedgehog (pencil and notebook) in some sort of position for play than the hedgehog crawls away, the doubled-up soldiers get tired of being hoops and disappear, while the flamingo looks up with a puzzled expression and the would-be player has to laugh. A baby, at least, doesn't disappear with such suddenness as a two year old, although he may well, as the hedgehog, crawl away.

In electing to study a baby the most important person to consult about making the study, and about the baby himself, is his mother. Something has already been said about the general willingness of mothers to have their babies observed and behaviour recorded. Some further advice, however, may be useful. The belief of any normal mother is that there is no baby like her own. This happens to be literally true and despite the fact that all babies (being of the same human kind) do go through stages of growth at roughly the same rate, and do have more in common with other babies than they do with older children or chimpanzees, each one is individual, and what his mother has to say about him is invaluable as evidence. To talk of him to the sympathetic listener is a great joy to almost every mother. The work of the Newsons (*Patterns of Infant Care in an Urban Community* and *Four Years Old in an Urban Community*) is a delightful example of how willing and how helpful are ordinary mothers to those who are undertaking a serious study of children. In spite of her student status, the novice observer has no less serious a purpose than the professional investigator, and will be accepted by mothers as such. Attention to the hints and advice throughout this book, about making sensible and courteous overtures to parents of children it is wished to study, should obviate any real problems of communication or relationship with families.

Although it is true that each mother intuitively responds to the unique nature of her child, while allowing for his common humanity, and loves to talk about him, it is also true that most are somewhat reluctant to admit their partiality. There seems to be a strange conspiracy, especially noticeable among the peoples of these islands and of some parts of the United States, to deny the beauty, charm, interest and sheer lovability of one's own child. Mothers deprecate their babies, sometimes going to the lengths of extravagant praise of someone else's child in an apparent effort not to appear too partial to their own. We have only begun to appreciate how extraordinary this is in the last few years. Such deprecating behaviour goes against all the nurturing instinct of a mother—which should ensure that every baby in the most vulnerable year of life, at least, has a partial, admiring and caring mother to give him confidence and trust in his own powers. It must be very difficult for very young children to believe in themselves as unique, worthwhile, trusted and trustworthy persons if their mothers are shy or doubtful about conveying this 'message' to them. It must be difficult to appreciate how greatly and deeply he is loved and wanted if a child's mother constantly worries about how he must appear to the neighbours, or whether she will seem 'soft' to other people if she demonstrates her affection. People in other parts of the world must be forgiven if they sometimes believe that the British don't much like their children. Mothers hesitate to demonstrate affection (although this is less true than it was only ten years ago); babies who stand up in their prams get smacked; toddlers who run to adults with complaints are often told 'not to tell tales'; teachers, even in nursery and Infants' schools retain, most stubbornly, the sanction of corporal punishment; and it does sometimes look to the observer from less severe societies as though an early start on reading is more important to parents than their small child's emotional, intellectual or even physical health.

Schools and clinics have too often been major culprits in this conspiracy of coldness, presenting a curiously unreal model of childhood to doubtful young mothers, in which neatness, obedience, cleanliness and a sort of slick cleverness are the most desirable features. As no real child of normal capacity is neat, obedient, clean or clever, all at one time, if ever, some faint defensiveness, as well as a deprecatory attitude about her child, is usually evident as one approaches a mother to ask if one may observe her baby or young child.

Sensing the slight tension in their mothers, even very young children 'play up' a little when a stranger comes into the home, and the student should bear this in mind. She should bear in mind, also, what has been written above about the attitudes and expectations of a large part of our society—she is, perhaps, the spearhead of a new generation, that will not let itself be persuaded that being cold, or undemonstrative, or punitive, or ambitious for young children is an acceptable and helpful way to start them off in life. She may be, in the warmth of her own personality, a very real factor in breaking down a mother's doubts and reservations about her effectiveness as a mother, and releasing her into easy and affectionate chat about (and to) her baby or toddler. On friendly, non-judging and easy terms, even the youngest and least experienced student will notice that a mother soon stops patting cushions, putting things away, apologizing for the battered furniture and murmuring uneasily about the difficulty of 'keeping things nice' or 'as we'd like them to be' in a home where there are young children. Every home where babies and young children—and older ones, too—are truly 'at home' is likely to be somewhat untidy, a little shabby, full of small flurries of noise, and odds and ends of nappies, plastic toys, half-eaten biscuits and evidence of domestic chores abandoned while some minor crisis is sorted out. Not even the most intelligent and 'organized' woman escapes the chaos that small children can create—unless, that is, she is determined that her house is of more importance than their childhood. Despite many stories of such mothers (usually 'on new estates') the writer's experience is that they are mercifully rare, and that most homes of children are, to a greater or lesser degree, much as described here. Whatever the home is like, however, it is no part of a student visitor's job to comment or criticize. She is a guest in the house (with a job to do, it is true) and without the extension of that hospitality could not get on with a very important part of her training.

ii

Having found a mother willing to accept her into the house in order to study a baby (or, of course, older child) there are important steps to be taken before the first recording session

24

can start. It is essential that some straightforward information about the child be noted:

Forename (no surname must be recorded—see below)
Date of birth
Sex
Position in family
Whether both parents are living in the house
Whether anyone else shares the home, e.g. grandparent or lodger

It is obvious that even a simple question about family members could be tactless—the novice should be very careful to find out by acceptable indirect means (this does not include 'asking around' in the neighbourhood) if there are any unusual circumstances which make the asking of a particular question tactless or tasteless. Go without the information rather than embarrass or annoy a parent! Other questions are permissible in this preliminary search for information about the baby, but, again, only if it is fairly obvious that they will not give offence:

Whether the birth was normal
What was the reaction of older brothers and sisters to the new baby
What the mother herself thinks of the baby's progress

In most cases there is hardly need to ask such questions, as almost every mother is willing to chat about such things. The problem for the student may be when—and whether—to write down much that is told her as the mother is talking. With the exception of date of birth, and names and ages of other children in the family, it is probably wiser to make mental rather than actual notes, and to write down any other information as soon after the visit as possible—so that the notebook does not seem to 'come between' visitor and mother. The record must be made very soon, though, while information is fresh in mind. Decisions about whether to write down what is said, how much and how obviously, really have to be made by the student in the light of her own common sense and sensitivity. It is often surprising to the novice that all sorts of quite intimate information comes tumbling out in the relaxed

25

atmosphere of a woman's own kitchen and with a friendly listener. Even that visitor's youth will often be no bar to such confidences; and this brings us up against the problem of confidentiality.

One of the key differences between being in a profession and being in trade or services of other kinds is that the professional has to hear and keep to herself a great deal of confidential information. It is true that many a workman doing a job in someone's house may hear and see much that the householder would not wish to have repeated outside. But such a workman is not there specially to be given such information; and he has no special understanding, stated or taken for granted, between him and the householder about the giving and receiving of it. He is not seeking it, above all, in order to do his job.

The student of children, on the other hand, is in the house in order to gather information that will forward her understanding of the way in which children grow and learn. She needs all the information she can get legitimately in order that she may, eventually, do her job of teaching, nursing or childcare more effectively. But there must be a clear, though unwritten, understanding between student and parent that all information gathered about the private life within a family (no matter how simple, harmless and ordinary most of this may seem) is absolutely confidential. We should all be outraged if the information given to our doctor, nurse, solicitor or priest, in order that he or she could do properly the job expected of them, were passed on to someone else, or made the subject of social chat. Right from the start it is wise for all those concerned with teaching and caring for other people's children to set for themselves the same strict rules about confidentiality as are set by other professions. (Apart from the moral obligation involved, there is the point that if groups of people wish to be treated as professionals they must be seen to behave like professionals, and not be known as persons who will gossip about the home and family circumstances of their 'clients'.) There are one or two exceptional circumstances under which an observer may feel that to keep complete silence may be to endanger the well-being of a child or children. Such rare occasions, and acceptable professional behaviour in the face of them, are dealt with at the end of this chapter. Generally speaking, it is essential that even the most ordinary-seeming information be treated as given in confidence.

To this end, the surname and address of the child being studied should not be recorded in any notebook or file used in connexion with child-study. Notebooks can be left on buses, or lying open in places where people known to the family may notice a name or comment. Every child studied, as every parent, teacher and school involved, must be given the safeguard of anonymity. It will be noticed that in a vast literature on child development no child, or even street, can be identified by name. The value (and validity) of investigations and reports is not in the least diminished by such a practice. Indeed, if mothers knew that they or their child might be named in print it is highly unlikely that they would be as generous as they have normally been in welcoming investigators and student visitors into their homes.

Adverse comment of any kind must also be avoided. It may be that some parental practice strikes a student as less than wise—but it is not her place to record this in writing, any more than it is to discuss it with fellow-students or anyone else. Practices which puzzle or perturb must be kept 'in the head', and may be discussed only in the privileged situation of the tutorial session; and only then with the honest intention of seeking enlightenment.

iii

Having established friendly relationships with a mother, and given her assurances of confidentiality, it is important to make one or two visits before actually recording a child's behaviour. During the course of these visits the practical information, as suggested above, will be collected. There is more, however. It is essential that the mother come to understand that the

27

observer does not want any special arrangements made for her visits. As has already been said, the relative untidiness or shabbiness of a home is irrelevant to child-study, and by having a cup of tea, chatting to other children in the home, and so on, the visitor conveys that at least no special tidying or cleaning is needed for her. With luck, she will end up in the kitchen or other general living-room on the first visit; if she doesn't, she ought, by her warmth and ease, to have got herself out of the 'best' room and into the usual living quarters by the end of that visit—or at the very beginning of the next.

Another matter affecting the naturalness of the situation for the baby or young child is the presence of other members of the family. If they are usually part of his 'scene' they must remain so. The observer must intimate that she does not expect granny to be sent upstairs, or a four year old to be banished to the garden or yard (he'll keep coming back, in any case), or the insurance man pushed out quickly, when he is patently used to staying for a chat with mother and a bit of fuss with the baby. Whether the presence of such members of his family make the recording of behaviour a little more difficult or not, really does not matter. If they are banished, the child's behaviour is no longer 'normal'. He is used, perhaps, to interaction with his grandmother, older brother or sister, visitor, and to be quite alone with mother may be an artificial situation for him. In any case, if the home, however, untidy or shabby, however full of others, suits the baby—it is good enough for the observer. For the child this is where 'it is all happening', and this is what it is wished to observe.

Finally, in one of these preliminary visits the student will somehow convey that she doesn't mind babies being a bit grubby. If a mother feels that she has to bathe and change a baby or small child before the observer starts work, it is possible that the relationship needs a little more time to develop, in order that the mother gets over her slight disquiet at the normal state of her child. The plain fact is that no normal baby or young child, leading an active, exploratory life (as all should), stays very clean for very long. The student is there to record his normal behaviour, not to take his photograph for the family album. She should be able to convey as much to the mother by her own friendly acceptance of life as it is, and babies as they are.

iv

Much of what has been said above about ordinarily courteous approaches, confidentiality and avoidance of having special arrangements made applies with equal force to observation in nurseries, schools and play groups. There are, however, obvious differences.

Visits to such institutions are arranged by the college, and it is most important that students do not make unilateral approaches to such places. The pressures on every place which caters for young children, from day nursery to primary school, are now very great. One small nursery school may be asked, in the course of a term, to accept two NNEB students, a small group of student-teachers on an observation visit, a final practice student-teacher, several overseas visitors, and perhaps one or two advanced diploma students pursuing an investigation into nursery education. That such schools go on shouldering this burden of training says much for the generosity and concern of the staffs. It is not acceptable for any student to make unilateral approaches, even if she is known at the school. It is difficult for a head teacher or superintendent to say 'no' to such a request—while saying 'yes' may quite gravely overload a staff already carrying a heavy training load. All placements in institutions simply must be made through the college. Restraint in such matters is yet another valuable professional habit which might as well be learned from the beginning of training.

No doubt college tutors will give their students wise briefing on sensible behaviour in other people's establishments, and it is unnecessary here to say more than that one should behave at all times with courtesy, consideration and respect for confidences. It is true that some habits and practices of some of our elders and betters may not be such as we should wish to emulate. The lesson to learn here is this: *When I am in charge as a qualified person, let me remember not to do this.* From even the most undesirable habits and practices there is much for the novice to learn, and it is wiser and in the end much more fruitful to ask *What should I do instead?* and *Why should I do it differently?* and *How do children respond to this?* rather than grumble, rage or weep. Most people in most nurseries and schools are skilled, helpful, efficient, and kind to children. If a student is unfortunate enough to have experience of poor practices by qualified persons she should, at least, ask if she may work in another kind of establishment on the next occasion of practical work.

Child-studies in school are obviously easier to make than in a home, in that there is a lot going on, and a student sitting with a notebook is not as obvious in a classroom as she is in a kitchen. The more difficult part of the task in a group of children is keeping a lively three, four or five year old in sight. Good sense must be used here. No child is going to be unaware for long that he is being observed if the observer follows him about, and tactful positioning, acceptance that several short studies rather than one longer one may be necessary, and willingness to leave the recording at short notice are needful.

Understanding between college and school staffs about the making of child-studies should have been arrived at long before the student starts her practical work. It is tiresome for a nurse or teacher to be told in the middle of a busy session that the student from whom she was expecting help with some activity is going to remove herself for ten or twenty minutes to observe a child. Some agreement should be arrived at not only between college and nursery or school but between the adults with whom the student is working and herself about a regular time during the day during which she will not be expected to involve herself with the ongoing work of the group. As far as possible, this period should be in a 'free play' session. It is not helpful to student observers to be given time only when young children are asleep, listening to a story or otherwise being static or 'directed' in activity. While some good observations may be made at such times it really is important for most of each study to be of a child in as free-choice a situation as possible. It is not necessary to ask for more than half an hour, although ideally an hour, from each day spent in the establishment in which to make studies of children. The job is so essential to understanding that such time is usually most generously given.

A vexed point arises about files and notebooks kept during practical work in nursery or school. Some head teachers take the view that such records are for the student's guidance alone, and are matter between her and her tutor. Others like to read every word, and add their own comments. Yet others appreciate a look over the notes if offered. Some tutors use the file as a teaching source during regular tutorial sessions, putting minimal comment on it during visits; others do not see it until the end of the practice; yet others write all over it, but do not use it in tutorial. The first of these courses is probably the best one. It is embarrassing for a student with a head teacher who reads every word in the file to know that the tutor's remarks will also be read by the head teacher. Consultation and agreement between student, tutor and head is the ideal—but, too often, the student is left out of this consultation, and is uncertain what her notebook is really for. As far as child-studies are concerned, she should follow the rule of anonymity given above. Surnames are not necessary for her record, even though she may have a group (or class) list in another file. Adverse comment simply must not be recorded, as already intimated. Head teachers and others can be very touchy about what they may see as criticism of their establishments or staff—and what they may view as criticism many of us might feel was 'fair comment'. Nevertheless, 'if in doubt—don't write it down' is a good rule for the student. Heads have been known to telephone college principals in a rage because they have seen in the preamble to a child-study such a comment as: *Brian hates fat—great scenes when he is made to eat it* or *Karen kicked Mrs. X when told to come in and listen to a very dull story.* Perhaps the anger is understandable, for here is a student openly implying that some very dubious practices exist in the school, and this puts the less secure head on the defensive. Whether it should or not, and how far maturity should preclude such response is another matter. The novice observer is well advised to eschew written comment of this kind.

Studying children in nursery and Infants' schools presents any of us with a delicate problem: that the child's mother may not realize that her child is the subject of such close observation and recording, and that she may (for all we know) object to such scrutiny when she finds out—as, in almost every case, she will. Normally, there is no problem in practice. Mothers, in the writer's experience, have welcomed the practice of child-study among students, and been most helpful in adding information to that gathered directly in school. They have almost always said or indicated that they realize that teachers, nursery assistants and others in training for a career with children need, above everything else, real knowledge of real children. *They'll learn more from him than they'll ever learn from books!* said one mother, wryly, of two students who were combining to study at depth the day-long activities of her lively four year old son. *I'd had three when he came along, and thought I knew about kids . . . But he came up with things I'd never dreamed of, saucy little monkey!* she added. Mothers will tell students that no two of their children are alike; that watching them makes them wonder 'where it all comes from'; that all the child-rearing books they ever read (and a surprising number of mothers have read a good many) still didn't prepare them for half the things their children say and do. They take a lively interest, in fact, in this aspect of student training, and offer most generous information if approached in a friendly manner.

It is true, however, that mother-student relations have greater or lesser success and warmth according to whether the school itself has a tradition of ease and open-access with parents. Nursery schools almost all have excellent relations with parents. Infants' schools vary greatly—and there are still too many where mothers are not permitted to gather outside the door, much less come into the classrooms. There are even a few, still, where they are not allowed past the school gate. Under such circumstances it is unlikely that the student will be able to talk to the child's mother while she is in the process of making her study of him. She should most certainly not imply criticism of the school's less good practices in any way while she is there. Her college probably has little choice of school places for practice, and however aware she may be that schools where mothers of young children are unwelcome are not good models of educational or social practice she should not comment. What she thinks to herself, or says in the privileged situation of the tutorial, is another matter, and one for her tutor to help her make constructive rather than destructive in tone.

Although in most nursery and Infants' school situations, and in most day nurseries, it will be possible for students to have some contact with the mothers of the children they are studying, this (as in the case of personal approach to mothers, mentioned above) is by no means a right. Children may have to attend school from the age of five, as a statutory obligation, but they do not have to be in nursery schools at all—and in neither place has teacher or student a right (legal or otherwise) to quiz mothers about their children. Mothers may refuse help and information, it is hoped, without being labelled 'difficult' or 'obstructive'. Much depends on the friendliness of relations and the ordinary courtesy and good sense of the student. It should be pointed out, however, that a very few mothers may be truly difficult and obstructive, no matter how good the home–school relations in general and how tactful and courteous the student. Such mothers are more often ill than wicked; more often hurt than hostile; more often feeling inadequate than truly aggressive. Moreover, they almost always have 'difficult' children, of one kind or another—and if the student finds herself studying a really aggressive, withdrawn or otherwise deviant child it is reasonably certain that his mother will not be 'easy'. It is better for the novice to leave bad alone, rather than make it worse by asking for further information from a parent whom the school knows to be non-helpful.

In the case of the preschool playgroup, if it is one associated with the Preschool Playgroups Association (and some groups calling themselves 'playgroups' are not in such association, and may be rather dubious places), no questions of contact with mothers, or professional tensions about it, arise at all. The mothers themselves staff the good playgroup. National and regional advisers now arrange courses of high standard for those who work in them. Many of the PPA 'staff' are trained teachers, nurses and child-care workers. In working with such a group the novice has the advantage of being in daily and intimate contact with every mother whose child is in the group. Although not as yet officially approved as 'training' places for student teachers, NNEB students and others, there is no doubt that it is only a matter of time before these groups, so deeply embedded in the neighbourhoods they serve, and so well staffed by the parents of those neighbourhoods, offer a quite new kind of opportunity for child-study to the student. It is likely that they will be among the most helpful of all places in which to make a start on child-study.

v

It must here be said that, despite a general rule of discretion, there are one or two exceptions to the rule of confidentiality. If there is evidence (and it must be evidence, not hearsay of a dubious kind) that a child is being ill-treated, mentally or physically, then that evidence simply must be taken to a proper authority as soon as possible. For most students in training the 'proper authority' is the tutor to the course, or the principal of a college. Reporting of such a situation must be as factual as possible, written down with dates and as much detail as can be collected, and relayed as soon as possible to the proper authority. If there are witnesses or informants, their permission should be sought to quote and call upon them if necessary—but if it is refused it is better to go ahead and make the report, noting the refusal, than to risk not making it. The important place of the teacher and nursery nurse, child-care worker and social worker in reporting cruelty to children has been discussed in Clegg and Megson's *Children in Distress* (1968) and Webb's *Children with Special Needs in the Infants' School* (1967). The case of Maria Colwell, fully reported (1974) and much discussed, is a horrifying example of unwise policy, inefficient system and lack of realization, in many quarters, that those in daily contact with children often know more about them and are more likely to be right in their assessment of a situation than are occasional visiting 'officials'. An estimated five thousand children a year are badly battered in their own homes; an estimated seven hundred every year actually die of it. It is likely that many who teach or care for children will live a professional lifetime without meeting a single such case. On the other hand, anyone might meet such a case very early in her career, and it is for this reason that this exception to the rule of confidentiality is discussed here.

Other exceptions are: evidence of flagrantly improper practice in a school, resulting in distress to children, or in diversion of public funds. In such cases, again, the proper person to whom a sensible and detailed report should be made is the student's tutor or the college principal—who will know how to approach which responsible person in the local education authority. It cannot be too often stressed that such cases are very rare indeed, and even where they are found it is more than likely that some responsible person has already noted and reported the matter. Only faced with indisputable evidence of malpractice should a visitor in a school take the matter to tutor or principal; and certainly never, under any circumstances at all, voice suspicion or discuss something of such an order with anyone else. It is unfortunate that so distasteful a matter has to be mentioned at all; but in a book intended for those who have to train eyes and ears and minds to sharp observation of children it is just possible that such observation may, during training or after qualification, have to be put in the service of 'children in distress'.

To end this chapter on a more positive and encouraging note, however, it will soon become apparent to the would-be observer that the making of good contacts with mothers, teachers and children is not just a matter of luck. It is the reward of goodwill, warmth and respect for persons, allied with real caring for the career that has been chosen.

Summary

Mothers are normally delighted to talk about their children; encouragement to do so is served by courtesy and informality of approach.

Allowance should be made for our society's pressure on parents to appear cooler and less partial towards their children than they really are; acceptance of parents, children and homes 'as they come', and an absolute absence of any hint of disapproval, usually breaks down any artificial reserve on the part of mothers.

Simple, factual information should be sought at the first visit, but observers must be sensitive to questions that are impertinent or might cause distress or hostility.

A student's youth is often no bar to a mother's chatting about most intimate family matters. Such matters should not be put in the notebook at all—a jotting down, as soon after the visit as possible of any truly relevant information is all that is necessary.

From the start of child-study all observers should practise the strict professional rule of confidentiality in respect of what is seen and heard in homes and schools, nurseries etc.

One safeguard of confidentiality is anonymity—no child should be identifiable by reason of surname or address in notes and records, even to fellow-students.

It must be conveyed to parents, by friendly and informal means, that no 'special arrangements' need to be made for the observer's visits—tidying of rooms, banishment of other members of the family normally present etc. only serve to produce an abnormal situation for the child who is the subject of the study. This is the very opposite of what is needed.

In visiting schools and nurseries students should abide by arrangements made by their college. In no circumstances should unilateral approaches be made to such institutions.

Adverse criticisms of practices in schools etc. is not acceptable; a constructive view should be taken, even of practices which the student may privately deplore.

Good sense, and previous understanding between college and school or nursery staffs, should enable a student to make her observations of children at times, and in such a manner, as to be unobtrusive and non-obstructive in the day's routine.

Files and notebooks kept during practical sessions in schools and other establishments may be scrutinized by the head of the establishment, or they may not. Views on this are very variable. Every notebook should be such that scrutiny by the head or supervisor does not give offence.

Contact and relationships with mothers of children studied in nursery or school are necessarily dependent on the existing home–school relationships. It is wise to accept the limitations that are occasionally imposed—and to remember that no one has a right to study a child just because he is outside his home.

Rare exceptions to the rule of absolute confidentiality in regard to information about children are: If it is believed that a child is being ill-treated by parents in the home; if there is evidence of serious malpractice causing distress to children or improper use of public funds in school. In any such case, the proper authority for a student to report matters to is her tutor or college principal—never to fellow-students or parents or teachers in other schools. Any such report must be factual, with written notes of dates, incidents etc. if possible, and no 'hearsay' should be taken alone as evidence.

4. Recording Behaviour: the Specimen Description

i

The first recording session should, of course, be after good relationship with mother or school has been established and one, or even two, preliminary visit(s) made. On the day that full observations are to start the observer should have proper materials ready. These are simple enough—several pencils or ball-point pens, and a shorthand writer's notebook. To have only one writing implement is inefficient, as a pencil may break just as the action becomes fast and interesting, a ball-point pen run dry, or the baby simply remove either and refuse to part with it. The point of having a shorthand writer's book is more apparent after the first trial of observing a lively child; the sheer speed at which it is necessary to record makes even the turning of a conventional page a hindrance!

The notebook should be rapidly ruled up, in pencil, before the session. Such sectioning, as suggested below, makes for easier recording at the time and easier analysis of information afterwards. It is essential to have a LEFT HAND MARGIN about half-an-inch wide, in which to jot down the time as recording takes place; and a RIGHT HAND MARGIN of about two inches in which to write the language or sounds the child uses.

The first page of the notebook (and any subsequent page

on which a new session starts) should contain a note of the child's forename, date of birth and actual age in years and months—months and weeks, in the case of a child below one year—on the day of the study. This avoids later mental arithmetic and also 'fixes' in an observer's mind the age and stage she is observing. Record age in months and weeks thus: 4m. 2w. It is permissible to record age in months for a child over a year, and many American writers do this. However, converting 47m. or 55m. into years and months is a minor irritation, as we use the form rarely in this country, and it is recommended that age from the first birthday onwards be recorded thus:

1 : 3 or 2 : 00

Note that the use of the colon (:) is important. If we write 1·3 it means one year and three-tenths of a year, not one year and three months. Another acceptable way of writing exact age is:

1y. 3m. or 2y.

	Date of observation Child's name + date of birth	
	+ actual age	
	Short description of situation in which observation is being made.	
Time here	What is happening here	Vocalization here
↓	↓	↓

Time   10 mins

Actions.   Language

It may seem pernickety to enter into such detail about the simple recording of age, but surprisingly often a student's record of a child's age is ambiguous—and this can make meaningful discussion of her observations impossible. It is also likely that all the above forms of recording age will be met in the textbooks, and readers might just as well be familiar with them from the start. The novice should decide on the simplest and clearest system for her own use—and stick to it in all her notes and records.

The first page of a session of recorded behaviour should look like the diagram on page 39.

There is, of course, no need to head any subsequent page of the same session, but every page should be ruled with margins before any session—the speed at which recording has to be done precludes any chance of making margins while the session is in progress!

With tutorial guidance the observer should also decide on the length of time each specimen description will take: five, ten, fifteen or twenty minutes. Each gives a reasonably good specimen of behaviour from which excellent information can be gained. It is not recommended that the novice should try recording a child's on-going behaviour for more than ten minutes—indeed, it may be felt that five minutes is quite long enough, for a start. After some experience has been gained the longer periods may be tried; although it will be found that noting everything a child does for twenty minutes is a very exacting task and quite as much may be gained from two ten-minute sessions.

With such preparations and decisions made, the next somewhat difficult task, although it sounds easy enough, is remembering to jot down the times in the left-hand margin as recording proceeds. Ideally, the time should be noted at one-minute intervals. A stop-watch is usually recommended in older American texts—but this is clumsy to handle, has to be reset, and is an expensive piece of equipment beyond the resources of most students. The best and most reasonable equipment is a watch with a very clear face and a sweep-hand; and it is then necessary to train oneself to glance at it often and rapidly.

Certainly, a time-record is essential to observational methods of all kinds. In using the specimen description method, where anything from five to twenty minutes of behaviour is being recorded it is impossible to tell, unless time-intervals are recorded also, and fairly often, whether the behaviour falls within normal (and credible) limits or not. A six-page record, for example, may represent the rapid, lively play of a normal three year old for less than five minutes; or it may represent the abnormal play of a hyperkinetic (over-active) child for two minutes; or the somewhat lethargic behaviour of a slow-learning or not-very-well child for twenty. Without a time-record at short intervals it is not possible to tell, and no realistic interpretations can be made of the record. It is, moreover, important to know whether the activity came in bursts or whether it was steadily maintained through the period of the observation; and this can only be assessed if the passing of time is recorded by the minute.

Active 'play' and periods of seeming 'rest' are essential in all learning, but individual patterns of activity and pause are highly variable—probably from birth. Each of us has a characteristic 'rhythm' and it is important for those who wish to do their best for children to note what are the rhythms of individuals in their charge. Some are active for sustained periods, going at a steady pace, and resting or pausing for short periods; some 'go hard at it' for short bursts, and rest for short periods; some are very vigorous for short periods, and need long, almost 'dreaming' pauses. There are probably infinite variations. Patterns of active work or play and rest or pause vary, too, with the activity itself, some children 'sticking with' a sedentary activity such as puzzles or crayoning for sustained periods, while being 'short burst and short pause' people when engaged in house-play, outdoor activity etc. Some are the reverse. The need for careful recording of time during an observation session is thus a most important one in child-study.

Some Americans have used a tiny light-bulb clipped to the corner of the board on which the recording pad rests, which flashes at one-minute intervals, and this would seem an excellent idea so long as the light is shaded in such a way as not to draw the attention of a small child. The writer has not yet found anyone to make up such a device in a form lightweight and reliable enough to use in observational child-study—but some readers may be able to overcome the technical problems involved. A one-minute egg-timer type of device has been used by some students; but this has proved awkward to use as the recording pad or board has to be held at a steep angle for it to work, and remembering to reverse it is rather more difficult than remembering to glance at a watch. Kitchen 'pingers' are far too distracting to be of use, and the need to reset them precludes their being of any use in a busy session with a busy child.

ii

Decisions have to be made about which situations to record. Subject to unexpected happenings and opportunities in the home or the school, these are best made before visits. In the case of babies it is usually advisable to observe behaviour in three situations interesting and significant to the young child: free-play, bathtime and bedtime routine. It may not be possible to sample all three when a visitor to the home, but when it is possible to do so these are most rewarding situations. Free play in the case of a baby can be deceptively unvaried at first sight. It may seem to the novice as though the baby 'just lies there', seemingly doing very little. If he is awake, however, closer observation shows that he is moving eyes, clenching and unclenching fists, and feet, wriggling, making sucking movements with tongue and cheeks, momentarily catching sight of mother, observer or a moving object or light and perhaps going very still as he concentrates on it, moving his head in response to sounds (and it should be noted, which sounds), staring, and so on. All this activity is crucial to his development as a conscious being, able to learn. It can be noted which way he turns his head when put down to sleep, when he seems restless, when most peaceful, what stops him crying, and what response he makes to the sound, smell or sight of feeding preparations. As a child grows older his play becomes more complex—he reaches for objects before he can actually locate them in space and grasp them, he grasps before he learns to let go, he takes everything to his mouth (that most sensitive of exploratory senses) and examines it with mouth and fingers after locating it with eyes. Crying becomes different according to what is needed; sounds begin to be elaborate; a whole repertoire of 'nonsense' babble precedes real words. There is, in fact, a very great deal for the alert student to note in the apparently non-active baby who cannot yet sit up, much less crawl or walk.

Once sitting is attained, there is even more to note. How long can he sit? With or without support? Is the back arched, or rounded? What use does he make of the new-found skill? At the onset of crawling much more can be noted: Just how does he crawl? With one foot pushing (and which one)? With both feet pushing? On knees, or on his bottom? When a child can stand it should be noted what aids he uses, whether he is delighted with the skill, what he can see from an upright position—and what use he makes of this extended horizon. The free play period becomes more and more full of opportunity as walking and climbing become possible.

In being fed, whether by breast, bottle or in high chair with cup and spoon, there is obviously a lot of 'training' mixed with the free, exploratory behaviour. Both are interesting and worthwhile to note. In being bathed there are yet more dimensions of experience for the young child. Most babies, and older children, too, have a delighted response to water, as we all know, and play vigorously in the bath from the age at which they can sit up and pat the water. Splashing, patting, and later squeezing of sponges, trying to catch soap and soap-bubbles, floating and sinking soap-dishes, bath-toys and any other object found in the bathroom —all give babies and young children a wide range of skills to practise and a wide range of sensory experiences not easily found elsewhere.

Older children, from around the age of two, tend to make bathtime and bedtime routines social occasions—partly out of sheer sociability, partly (one suspects) in order to prolong the pleasure of playing with water and to delay the inevitable abandonment to bed and relative solitude. Bedtime routines are a study in themselves, involving as they do, highly individual rituals of all kinds from a careful look behind the curtains to a certain kind of story and a rhythmic incantation that passes for 'prayers'. The usual 'quiet' ending of the romp and noise is important for most children—and for their parents! The wise observer will depart with her notebook, downstairs, if not immediately out of the house, while mother or father 'settles' a child finally for the night. Over-excited children are a nuisance to themselves and to others in the house, and it is neither kind nor wise to let the fun of bathtime or pre-bedtime romp get to a pitch where a child has to be reproved or mildly punished—as can easily happen with a relative stranger in the house, for young children do tend to 'show off' in front of her.

In observing children of around four or five it is rewarding to observe the same situations but mealtimes become more sociable, and rightly so, so that it is harder to record what a child is doing and saying. He wishes to chat to the visitor, and should be allowed to do so. It would seem unnatural, in any case, to sit and watch an older child at meals, while writing down what he did in a notebook. Much more about children may be learned by joining with a family at a meal, and enjoying the company of the sociable child, than in just taking a specimen description of his behaviour in such a situation. There will, therefore, probably be more observations during free-play times and perhaps at bathtimes (which usually come to the same thing, in any case!) of a child between the ages of three and five than there will be observation of his mealtime behaviour. This can be noted, mentally, and recorded as notes, not specimen behaviour, afterwards.

In observing children in school or nursery the question of bedtime and bathtime observations does not arise. Behaviour at mealtimes, in the washroom and in putting on and taking off clothes can, however, sometimes be observed more discreetly in a large group of children than in a normal household. It is important, however, not to follow a child from playroom to washroom and then out of doors or back into the playroom. No child of any sense is likely to miss the fact that special attention is being paid to him, as has already been mentioned, and he will become silly, shy or sullen as he realizes what is happening.

In fact, no child ever should realize that he is being observed. The good observer waits for appropriate opportunity—and goes without a record for the time being if she suspects that a child is becoming self-conscious, or might become so in a particular situation. It is, after all, a relatively simple matter to study his behaviour during free-play on one day, his mealtime behaviour on another, and his response to washing and dressing routines on a third. Further information about him may be gained from his mother, if relationships with the school or nursery are good (in the playgroup, as already indicated, no problem arises in this connexion)—a point which has been discussed in Chapter 3 above. No matter whether information is forthcoming from a mother or not, every nursery or school has a record of a child's date of birth, and usually of his position in the family as well as of any special circumstances which it is proper for the observer to know in order to make sensible interpretation of her information. There is some information about children which some heads and supervisors would not think it proper to be given to anyone but the child's teacher (and some that she might be reluctant to pass on, even to the teacher or nurse), and such professional respect for confidences must be respected. The kind of information often in the head's file is that relating to fostering or adoption, or to a father's absence in prison. Such knowledge may or may not explain some puzzling aspects of a child's behaviour—but if it is not given, or a student is told that she may not look at a child's school or nursery record cards, she should accept this restriction with good, professional grace. If she

45

is given such information it goes without saying that it must be treated in absolute confidence, and not recorded for anyone else to read—possibly not even her tutor, but certainly no other student, nurse or teacher. 'Difficult family circumstances' is as far as any student should go in explaining or putting a tentative interpretation on a piece of recorded behaviour when in the tutorial group.

As much use as possible should be made of the free-play periods in nurseries, schools and playgroups. In these situations there is often more for a child to do, and more time for him in which to 'do his own thing' than there is in even the best home. Not least, there are many other children with whom he can interact—and the way he deals with social relationships is a major study in its own right. All this is more than compensation for the lack of other valuable information of a kind that is more easily gathered in a child's home. The student, in fact, must be prepared to make the very most of each situation—the intimacy of home and the relationships of child and family, or the busy, socially expansive life of the nursery or school group.

iii

It has to be acknowledged that even sound preparation and wise selection of situations in which to make observations will not make the task an easy one. Recording of on-going behaviour has to be done at breakneck speed, and even then no one of us, however proficient, can record everything a child does and says as it is happening. The use of shorthand does ease the job somewhat—but very few intending nursery assistants or teachers have this skill. However, anyone can develop some kind of rapid writing code that is legible after a session. For example, LH, RH, LF and RF are obvious ways in which to record which hand or foot is in action. 1F, 2F etc, can stand for which fingers are being used. Little symbols can be used for certain uses of the hand, e.g.

clenched fist   pincer grip   spread fingers

Such symbols as → R or L ← and ↑↓ record movements in space. Each observer should devise her own code, and use it until it becomes a habit. It is not helpful to devise a long and elaborate code. No one is going to remember dozens of symbols, even if she devised them herself and believed them to be very suitable ones. It is best to start with a few obvious ones, on the lines suggested above; others may suggest themselves as experience is gained. Some practice might be made on willing fellow-students, by recording their ordinary movements as they perform an everyday task, before making a start on the first observation of the selected child.

All recording of child behaviour should be in the present tense. The behaviour is, after all, being recorded as it happens, and not recollected afterwards (except in a few exceptional cases); it is thus likely to be more accurately recorded in words that reflect its immediate nature. Moreover, recording in the present tense gives a sense of involvement and immediacy to the observer and to any other reader looking through the records subsequently. An example of a two-minute observation will be found at the end of this chapter, before the summary.

iv

Even when excellent relations have been set up with the child, the mother and other adults in the home (or school), all sensible preparations of notebook and writing materials made, and such matters as a rapid-writing code devised, time recorded etc. there will be situations which the novice finds difficult to deal with unless she is advised in advance about possible courses of action.

47

Such a situation is that of the young child, whether in his own home or in school, who becomes aware of the unobtrusive observer and approaches her either to find out what she is doing or to invite her to join in his activity, admire his work or hear him read. The best course is to draw a line rapidly across the bottom of the last lines, jot down the time in the left-hand margin, and note (quickly) what kind of attention the child is seeking, e.g. *John grabs my pencil* or *Susan says 'I want to write like you'* or *Andrew asks 'Can you fix this wheel?'* The observer is there to study child behaviour as it is and as it happens, and a child's approaches to her for attention, out of curiosity or for everyday help are as much a part of his behaviour as the rest of his activity which does not involve her. While she is dealing with him it is obviously impossible to record the interaction—but this is one of the permitted exceptions to the rule that behaviour must be recorded as it happens. It is strongly advised that such interesting interactions be recorded, as accurately as possible, as soon after the event as possible, and in the past tense.

A useful device with very young children (i.e. from about one year to two) is to give them attention for a few minutes, and in so doing divert their attention to some other interesting pursuit, possibly with mother or other adult. With any child who 'wants to write' a simple explanation (*I'm doing some writing. Would you like to do some, too?*), together with the provision of a pencil or ball-point and some sheets from the back of a pad, provides a first-class opportunity to observe how the writing implement is used, what is drawn or scribbled, the direction and pressure of the strokes, the naming of what has been produced, and so on. With children of any age from three or four to seven or eight the explanation can be accompanied by a request *Draw me a man!* The resultant drawing can be retained by the observer (especially if she says how much she would like to keep it, when it will usually be bestowed with great pleasure as a gift), and is a most useful part of her record of the child's level of ability and understanding. There is even a means of assessing this level quite formally from a child's drawing of a man; but opinions vary as to the usefulness and accuracy of the measure, and tutorial guidance should always be sought before using a drawing to assess so-called intelligence. (See: Goodenough, *Measurement of Intelligence by Drawing*, 1926.)

In the case of a child interacting with the observer the very last thing to do is to send him away because his behaviour is being studied! This results in a crestfallen or cross child, whose natural tendency to socialize with a friendly adult has somehow, and in a manner he cannot understand, been found 'wrong'. The child is always more important than the record; and there will be ample opportunities to record his behaviour at times when he is unaware of or unconcerned with the observer.

The exceptionally deprived or anxious child might well approach the observer so often as to make objective study of his play and social relations with others quite impossible. In the first place, it is not advisable for a novice to study such a disturbed child; in the second, the needs of the child for attention and cherishing from a virtual stranger really are more important than written record. If such a child had been selected for study very careful notice should be taken by mother or teacher of this behaviour. It is not enough to say *Oh, he just wants attention!* Of course he does. The really important question is *Why?* Normally loved and secure children soon lose interest in someone, however friendly, who is quietly going about her own business, and will turn soon to the much more interesting business they have with age-mates, toys or materials. It is the child with a special need for love and reassurance who cannot leave the stranger alone, and such a child, however much the observer may wish to and even be able to give him extra attention on some occasions, is not the best sort of subject for a child-study by the novice. It would be wise to start another study of a less demanding child, and give extra attention to the disturbed child on other occasions.

Another sort of intervention that often puzzles students is that of mother or teacher with a child. Should such intervention be recorded? Discouraged? Left out of the record while the activity before and after it is recorded? The answers are, again, those of good sense. So long as the preliminary talks with mother or teacher have established that no special arrangements are to be made for the observation periods, that no child is expected to be 'put through his paces' for the observer, and that it doesn't matter what he does so long as it is easy and natural to him, it is unlikely that undue intervention from adults will occur. It is true that there are very anxious mothers who will incline to tell their young children what to do or say, give him 'special' tasks or toys in order to show the observer that he or she is really clever or capable, or even play with him in a very directing sort of way. This tendency should be picked up by the observer in preliminary visits, however, and no observations should be made until the mother is so relaxed that such undue interference with the child is felt to be quite unnecessary. There are some teachers, too, who seem to feel that any nóisy, so-called silly or slightly unorthodox behaviour by children in the classroom will be thought by the observer to reflect on their own efficiency. They 'lose face', in their own eyes at least, if every child is not behaving as some sort of model infant. Again, it is only by her own relaxed friendliness, her modesty, and her genuine desire to just look at children as they are (which she conveys to the anxious teacher more by manner than by words) rather than as ideal beings, that will prevent little flurries of interference and over-direction on the part of such a teacher.

Allowing that good sense, warmth and sound preliminary work has been done, there will still be natural interactions between child and adult while the observations are being made. No child lives in a sterile and artificial world where he plays and works without other human contact (which is, of course, why some people regard the experimental psychologist's work in the laboratory with some doubt as to its relevance to a child's everyday life), and his responses to others are part of the behaviour we wish to observe. The only requirement in the recorded material is that it should

probably especially likely if these older children are themselves only four to six years of age; children of seven and above tend to be either bored by what the observer is doing (it being a relatively non-active pursuit, in their view) or very proud of the small sibling, and more likely to 'show him off' than to be resentful. The fours to sixes, and even three year olds in a less artful manner, will sometimes tease the baby until he cries or becomes very angry, or use his playthings with the bland excuse *He can't do it properly—I'm showing him.* Both manoeuvres are likely to divert the observer's attention from the baby to the older child—which is the object of the exercise. Attempts to prevent this sort of intervention by reproof or wheedling will almost certainly result in even greater efforts on the part of the resentful older child to detract interest from the baby. Depending on the age of the other child the wise observer will either enlist the mother's help in giving the disgruntled or over-helpful older sibling something much more interesting and challenging to do, or supply pencil and paper so that he, too, can 'record'. With children of around seven and over the observer can actually take them into her confidence, explain the purpose of her visits and the use of child studies, and enlist their help—whether that 'help' involves departing elsewhere for short periods, writing down what they know or think about the little brother or sister (invaluable data can be obtained this way!), or sitting quietly with their own pursuits or beside the observer, being a co-recorder. Good nature and understanding of children should prevent that most unhelpful of all responses from older siblings—jealousy and resentment. More generous older children then tend to interact naturally with the younger one, on appropriate occasions, as they do when the observer is not in the house, and this kind of interaction can be recorded as can that of the adults, in brackets, as part of the ordinary stimulus that the young child experiences every day of his life.

A student of child-behaviour is a student of all children's behaviour. Much of what is noted in the interaction of brothers and sisters, their relations with parents, neighbours' children, cousins and other relatives is an enormous aid to understanding when a student becomes teacher, nursery nurse, child-care worker or playgroup leader. Such information, gathered within families as the more controlled and detailed study of one child proceeds, gives the observer another kind of data. It should be noted as soon after visits as possible (in note-form, not with any attempt to time it or recall minute detail), and added to the store of information that every worker with children builds up over the years.

No two families are exactly alike; no set of brothers and sisters behave towards each other in the same way; no stereo-types of what it is like to be 'older brother', 'big sister', 'the baby of the family' or 'the middle one' are very helpful. Only by noting how individual children interact with each other and with the family at large can we get some idea of whether there are patterns of relationship common to us all, or not. This noting of sibling interaction is particularly interesting and valuable for the student who is herself an only child. There does seem to be, among only-children-grown-up, a belief that 'having a sister' or 'being a brother' etc. means the same thing for most children. Involvement in a family or two, while making child-studies, and sensitivity to inter-action between siblings, soon demonstrates that this belief is far from the truth.

It must always be remembered that the experience is one of personal relationships and intimate involvement to the family being visited. The intending teacher, nursery nurse or other worker with children has a moral as well as a profes-sional duty—and that is to regard the family whose child(ren) she is studying as much more than a source of case-material or data for her case-work. The student may be required to make several studies in homes and schools during her course, but to each family or school staff she is an individual who is genuinely interested in them and in particular children, not a recording-machine which switches on and off regardless of family and other needs. Obviously, she cannot go on visiting each family and school she has known and been made wel-come in for years afterwards when she has so much else to do. But her withdrawal from the situation should be as thoughtfully considered, as kind and as considerate of persons as were her preliminary visits. To snap her notebook shut after the final recording session, or the last day of a school practice, as if to say *That's that! Thanks for the data!* is as hurtful as it is graceless. Another visit or two might be made, at longer intervals; a family might be invited to a college function; several students might co-operate in offering some simple hospitality to 'their' families. And it is to be hoped that every college depending on schools for its essential training of students offers regular hospitality to the staffs of 'practice' and 'observation' schools, nurseries and the like; with full involvement by the students who have 'lived with' the staff and not only by the principal and senior members of staff over an elegant sherry—pleasant as this is as an extra 'thank you'.

Finally, it is possible that many mothers and teachers would appreciate knowing something of what a student does with all the notes and observations she makes. In many cases, some analyses of the raw data are 'safe' enough to be shared with parents and teachers. There are, however, very anxious mothers who may well be upset by even the most sensible and objective comparison of their child with textbook 'norms', since they will not realize the broad band of what is 'normal'. There are teachers who may become anxious if they think that their behaviour has been studied, in studying children's, and not understand that this is almost inevitable and is certainly not adversely critical in intent. It is hard enough for students, who will be professionals and able (it is hoped) to see the whole picture, to remain objective about their data. It is almost impossible for parents, and very difficult for some teachers—who perhaps ought to be better at it, but who simply are not. Any interesting information which tends to make mother or teacher feel more confident in herself, and gives her more insights into how children grow and learn and behave, is proper to give. No other should be given. In the writer's view it is only courteous, and will only add to the common store of knowledge, to indicate that there are proper and useful follow-ups from observation and that these are invaluable in the training courses. But students would be wise to abide by tutorial guidance in discussing their work with parents and teachers, and at no time to breach faith with either the families, schools or college staff by tactless or over-zealous discussion of what uses were made of the collected data. It is possible to treat parents and others as partners without discussing with them everything done in tutorials, seminars, written work or analyses based on the child-studies.

Example of Specimen Description based on observation for two minutes of a two and a half year old.

| 26.9.74 | Julie | d.b. 29.3.72 age 2:6 |

| 9.37 a.m. | J. is coming out of her house on to the unmade road by a river-bank, where a slightly muddy footpath, grass, stones, a small clump of trees and two parked cars present a varied set of stimuli (or hazards). Observer is sitting on step of house some fifty yards from Julie's. | |
| | J. comes down steep stone steps sideways, R.F. down, followed by L., looking down at feet. Action repeated for each step. Wobbles slightly as bottom is reached and both feet on uneven gravel. Walks with stomping gait, arms outstretched, R.H. pointing, index finger out, to footpath, Stops. Lowers arms, points R.H. index finger at feet. Turns from waist, feet still | Urrgh! Ibet! |

planted firmly and looks towards observer. Swings L. arm out and moves feet to start walking along path. (Her family dog, Jess, comes out, passes her.) J. staggers, waves both arms at dog. Shouts: Quickens pace, firm stomping gait, R. arm, extended, index finger points towards dog. (Tractor crosses bridge, very noisy.) J. stops. Stares hard towards bridge. Feet apart. Points R. index finger towards bridge. Frowns. Picks nose briefly R. index finger. Mouth down at corners. (Tractor is very noisy, but noise dying away.) J. turns from waist, finger in mouth, looks towards house. Starts walking towards observer. Solemn face, arms swinging. [Obs: You're going for a walk, are you?] Stamps R. foot. Points towards dog with R. index finger. [Obs: No, she's not a bad girl. She's just sniffing the tree, like my dog does. Where's Mummy? Obs stands up.]	Tum waw, Tum wi' Jeb! Igo da! Igo da! Tum waw! Car-car go! Tum waw! Wi' Jeb—ah! Seeba' gel. See's away.

9.38 J. stomps past observer, stops, holds rail of rustic fence, looks at it. Curls fingers round rough bark, pats it, stares closely at it. Looks

up quickly, waves R.H. at dog (now rustling about in trees and long grass), leans over low rail. Kicks foot in mud, makes grimace.	You tum! Urrgh!
[Obs: Yes, it's muddy this morning! Mind your nice red boots!]	
J. stares down at feet.	Iboos!
Obs. notices deep mud on path further along, and moves towards J. to head her off, or lift her over. Asks: Where's Mummy?]	See's away.
J. reaches deep mud and puddle. Stops, looks down. Bends stiffly from waist, feet straddled. Points with R. index finger, puckers face, looks up at obs.	Iboos! Itup!
[Obs: No, I don't think you're stuck! Here, up we come! Obs. lifts J. out of puddle.]	
J. puts arm confidently round Obs. neck, twists head to look towards her own house. Wriggles and waves L. arm and hand. She is lowered on to dry part of path.	Jeannie tum
[Obs. scribbles in notebook, leaning it on bonnet of car.]	Car-car!
J. stares then turns to aunt who has come out of house. Breaks into smile, turns clumsily but quickly, runs with staggering gait towards bridge.	
[Aunt catches up with her,	

	says Come on now, in the garden with you!] J. stumbles on a tussock of grass. Sits down suddenly, legs outstretched, looking up at aunt, and then back at obs. Laughs. Leans sideways. resting R. palm on path, levers herself up by using hand and feet in semi-crawl position. Staggering run	
9.39	towards house, shouting.	Tats—no! No tats!

Much that might be called typical of a two and a half year old is caught in this specimen of behaviour for even so brief a period as two minutes. The manner of coping with steps, the slight stagger in the gait, the excited waving and pointing, the immediate response to a loud or unfamiliar noise (the signs of slight anxiety as the tractor passed should be noted), the independence, the already learned 'taboo' on getting dirty, the bossiness towards the dog, the initiation of a chasing game, and so on, are commonly found in children of this age. But there are ways in which Julie is expressing a highly individual way of 'being two'. Her language is slightly atypical, for example (to find out in which way—consult tables of normative items!), and so is her casual, even complacent, seeming acceptance of her mother's absence. The presence of two much older brothers (of eight and ten years, respectively) is reflected—as the reader cannot hear, however—in tones of voice, and her mannerisms also are quaint imitations of older, boyish ones, on occasions.

Note that no interpretations are given in the actual description of the on-going behaviour. This is important. It might be legitimate to think that Julie was, momentarily, frightened by the very loud rattle and roar of the tractor—but we cannot know for certain, and it is most unacceptable to write such things as 'Julie is frightened by the tractor' or 'She knows she must not get dirty in the mud', while the actual behaviour is being recorded. The only legitimate interpretations are of the kind that the present writer has given in the preceding paragraph—cautious assessments based on the child development literature, past experience of many two years olds, and very careful scrutiny of a very detailed specimen of behaviour. Even when common sense suggests that Julie was actually looking at the dog, or at the tractor the observer used the word 'towards' dog or tractor. It is never certain that a child is actually looking at what we think he or she is, and it is thus more objective and restrained to say 'seems to be looking' or 'looks towards' or 'appears to stare at his mother'. By such meticulous means we can avoid the dangers of interpreting from a child's on-going behaviour what we want, or expect, or think we ought to see.

Summary

Observers should be provided with a shorthand writer's notebook and more than one pencil or ball-point pen.

Child's forename, date of birth and exact age on the day of each observation should precede each record.

Age should be recorded simply and in one of the conventional ways—keeping to the same style throughout.

Notebooks should be ruled up with small left-hand and larger right-hand margin before each session, to enable more rapid recording, and easier subsequent analysis.

The length of time to be used as a specimen of behaviour should be decided in consultation with the tutor—and with regard to the novice's lack of skill to start with. Ten minutes is probably quite long enough before experience is gained; twenty minutes is usually considered long enough to get a good specimen of behaviour, even by experts.

Time should be recorded at one-minute intervals, using the easiest means possible—usually a watch with a clear face and a second-hand. If time is not recorded the specimen becomes meaningless.

Situations to observe, and from which good specimens of normal behaviour can be taken, are free play sessions, bathtime and bedtime. Sense should be used in deciding when and how to take advantage of these situations.

Situations for children in school obviously cannot include bathtime and bedtime routines—but many other sorts of situation are excellent substitutes for them.

It is important that a child in school should not become aware that he is 'being followed' from room to room, as a student obtains specimens of his behaviour. He can be observed in a different situation on a different day.

Some sort of rapid-writing code should be devised by students, and kept very simple, before starting recording.

All recording of on-going behaviour should be in the present tense.

There are many wise ways of dealing with the situation when the child being observed approaches the observer, and distracts her from noting his behaviour.

Interaction with mother, other children and persons in the home is natural to the child, and should not be discouraged. All such interaction should be recorded by putting the part of the mother or other person in brackets.

The behaviour and responses of other children in the home (or class) of the child being studied are of use and interest to the student of child behaviour. They can be jotted down, after the session, in note form.

A courteous and considerate 'weaning away' from a family or school where the observer has been collecting information is essential, and must, somehow, be attained.

What is done with the records and notes is a matter of interest to parents and teachers alike. Only such material as will be encouraging and non-offensive must be shared in this way, and tutorial guidance in the matter is strongly advised.

5. Choosing Themes and Selecting Designs for Child Study

i

When beginning to study children by observing them it is important that every possible action and word of a baby or child should be recorded while it is happening. In practice, of course, no observer can record at such a speed, or have so sharp an eye and ear as to put down literally everything that happens in the course of even a few minutes. Even an active baby, who cannot yet walk or talk, is using eyes, hands, legs, toes, tongue, small facial muscles and vocal chords as he feeds, responds to other persons, explores objects and materials and makes his wants known. The older child, on his feet and with some language at his command, is in ceaseless interaction with his total environment of space, toys, furniture, people and materials—unless he is asleep. Even then the good observer will record turnings, twitchings, smiles, eyelid flutter and mutterings which indicate that the mind is very far from inactive during long periods of sleep.

Despite the realistic appreciation that not every move and sound can be recorded—unless by a cine-camera—every beginner should have as an ideal the recording of every move. This at least prevents her from developing the bad habit of recording only what seems 'interesting' or 'significant'. We cannot know what is significant unless we try to record fully whole sequences of behaviour, with nothing left out. It has already been pointed out that prejudgement of 'what matters' leads to dull, sentimental or dangerously stereotyped records. What is essential as a basis of child-study is a set of studies of individual children, of different ages and sex, with no pre-decided theme. Such studies serve to give the novice practice in close observation, exact recording and (later) analysis of a rich and varied specimen of normal behaviour; they alert her to the enormous individual differences to be found among the most ordinary of normal babies and children; and they indicate to her some of the many aspects of child-response and child-behaviour that reward further, and more predecided. study.

Some of the themes which may particularly interest a student who has made several studies are:

Locomotor development and skills: when and how children learn to sit up, grasp, manipulate objects, stand, crawl, walk, climb; what sort of neuro-muscular co-ordination is needed to run without stumbling, ride a tricycle, cut with scissors, guide a pencil—and at which age, approximately, most children achieve such skills; whether differences between boys and girls are observable in such development, or differences according to facilities, encouragement and provision at home.

Emotional growth: confidence, shyness, changes of response with age, ability to persist in a task, tolerance to frustration, irritability, placid behaviour, and so on, are indicators of what Gordon Allport (in *Pattern and Growth in Personality*: Holt, Rinehart and Winson, 1963) has called 'the internal climate' of an individual; how far such emotional responses vary, even in one child, according to place, time and people, or change with maturity.

Social development: which is closely connected with both locomotor ability and emotional 'tone'—at which ages and stages children can cope with a small group, a larger group, with strangers; how they resolve small conflicts; whether they co-operate, lead, follow or play alone when in a group; how

62

they respond to simple training in manners and independence, and which training approaches seem most fruitful at which ages.

Language development: which sounds are made first, and through which sequences of sound children develop recognizable speech, to whom they make overtures in words; what kind of sentences they make; what they use language for: demand? command? question? self-assertion? expression of thought? exchange of views? reassurance?; whether social class, racial or regional factors affect language development—and, if so, in which ways. What do young children talk about?

Intellectual development: which is inextricably associated with all the other aspects—curiosity, questioning, experiment, recognition of relationships between classes of animals, plants, people and things, persistence, concentration and ability to recall and recount happenings are all indicators of intellectual growth; at which ages do certain of these occur? are there differences by sex, social class or region, home experience or amount of nursery or school experience?

Every theme mentioned under one of the above headings might stand as the title of a major study. There is no need for a student to wonder whether she will be able to think of a particular aspect of child-development to study—a look over her previous studies of individual children will suggest something that particularly interests her. A glance through the above themes might alert her to an incident or two in her own records which would be interesting to study further. It is at this stage, and not any earlier, that more complex studies (*but still based on observational techniques*) may be undertaken.

ii

'More complex' as used above refers to a more complex design for child-study, not to more complex themes or more elaborate methods. Complex themes such as emotional deprivation, development of particular concepts, response of handicapped children etc. are really best left to specialists or to the very experienced investigator; elaborate methods, such as standardized testing, rating on attitude scales, observation under laboratory conditions, and so on, are not necessary or suitable 'tools' of investigation for most teachers or nurses, much less for the novice.

More complex design, however, is possible and desirable as a training course proceeds. It is desirable for students to work in pairs or small groups rather than alone, and to make all decisions about the theme to be studied, *before* they enter the nursery, school or other institution, i.e. the number of children they can handle, the form of recording and definition of terms they will use. Tutorial guidance is essential here, and should be available throughout the course of the study.

Cross-sectional studies of child behaviour are useful, and the design of such studies not beyond the competence of well-guided novices who have had previous experience of observational study of individual children. By 'cross-sectional' is meant here the study of a group of children who have age in common; who will be studied at a certain point in time; and about whom the same kind of information will be recorded. Students might decide that they were interested in the social interactions of two or of three year olds; or in the language of four year olds; or in the responses of children at certain ages to frustration; or the friendships of six or of seven year olds. No matter what the theme, the students would agree on how many children each of them may be able to observe, for what periods of time, within what total period. They would discuss which of the observational techniques described in the rest of this book would be most appropriate to their theme and the situation they will work in.

Most importantly, they would agree on what they will mean by the words they use. As examples: in looking at the social interactions of three year olds the student-observers must agree on what they mean by a 'quarrel'—a simple snatching of a toy? a push? a tantrum over another child's grabbing of a tool? or a sulky withdrawal? Is a 'friendly overture' going to mean the offering of a turn on the swing? a chatty monologue as a child plays beside another? a smile? a pat on the teacher's leg in passing? In studying intellectual aspects of development how is 'persistence at a task' to be defined? Will one observer feel that two minutes is a long period for a very young child, while another thinks that five minutes is not very long? And how is 'concentration' to be measured, even after it is defined? This is where the previous studies, the growing familiarity with textbook norms and, above all, sound tutorial guidance will prevent confused or inexact results from a lot of hard and conscientious work. One cannot go back and have a child live again a few minutes of his life. Once missed, that episode is forever irretrievable. It is sad for students to have to say, as they go over a morning's records, *I thought we weren't going to count that—John did it several times, but I don't remember exactly who to . . .* or *I didn't put down all the sounds they made, the nonsense words—I thought we just had to record real words . . .*

The outcome of a cross-sectional study will be many exact observations of one kind of behaviour or response on the part of a number of children of the same age, all the observations having been made within a limited period of time. Children's development is so rapid in the first five or six years of life that to return to the same sample of children a month later is to get a quite different sort of information, in most cases. It is essential that cross-sectional studies be undertaken either of all the children it is wished to study within not longer than a week or fortnight at most or of different groups of children whose chronological ages are the same. It is useless to collect data on what the same children were doing at, say, the age of 3y. 4m. and again a couple of months later at 3y. 6m. and call the study a cross-sectional one. Two months after the first study, if more information on the age-group (say) 3y. 2m. to 3y. 4m. is wanted it is necessary to select another group of children in this age-range and, of course, in the same situation.

Longitudinal studies, on the other hand, have the intention of studying changes which occur in time. They are essential if we wish to know at what speed and in which sequence children develop abilities and acquire skills. In longitudinal studies, having decided carefully (in the manner already described above) what it is that is to be studied, in which situations, units of time, by how many students, and so on, it is essential to decide the total length of the study. It is not advisable for the novice to try to monitor change over too short a period—unless the subjects of the study are babies in the first year or year and a half of life, when even the beginner can see very great changes in periods of time as short as a month or six weeks. In most cases it is advisable to take a school year (which, in practice, amounts to about ten and a half months, i.e. September to mid-July) or a full calendar year, and make observations at predecided intervals, of the same aspects of development, during that period. The outcome will be a collection of observations showing how certain abilities and skills have developed as growth and experience have occurred.

Another advantage of the longitudinal kind of design is that it can be used by one student, studying one child, throughout a substantial part of her course. It is the kind of record kept by some mothers who are particularly interested in the development of locomotor skills, language or other 'noticeable' phenomenon. Applied to a group of children believed to be at risk in a difficult situation—a poor neighbourhood, for example—or at risk by reason of suspected birth-damage, the longitudinal study may give clues, as each part is carefully scrutinized, to the beginnings of 'maladjustment' or learning difficulty. Comparison with longitudinal studies of children in more favoured situations or with no history of difficult births may throw out very clearly the kind of developmental 'gap' or deviancy which has to be compensated for or treated, as well as the stage at which it is likely to occur.

A combination of cross-sectional and longitudinal design is, of course, possible—although this is an exacting task, in terms of numbers of children and numbers of observations to be made over a fairly long period. It may be decided that the theme chosen by a group of students for study calls for both a fairly large set of cases at each age-interval and the plotting of change over time if it is to be fully rewarding. Language development often calls for such a study, and so does progress in developing number-concepts or acquiring the skill of reading. Because the design of such a study is complex it is not advisable for students to undertake it without previous experience of both individual child-study and some previous experience with either a cross-sectional study or longitudinal study, or both.

It is the responsibility of the tutor to give guidance in such an undertaking, as in all others. The rewards of a group undertaking of this order, however, are very great, and it might constitute a major part of the second or third year work in a training course. Since the combination of sound observation, good recording and familiarity with the different kinds of information to be derived from differently designed studies is crucial to success in professional investigations it is most important that aspiring teachers, nursery nurses and child-care workers develop some skill in these matters. More and more often, research teams based on universities and other such places now call on the people who are in daily charge of children to provide them, under guidance, with the data they need. This is a most welcome trend and one which will be well served by those in nurseries, schools and other places where children are gathered who appreciate what is needed because they have themselves made good and varied child-studies.

Summary

As detailed and full a record of a child's on-going behaviour as it is possible to make should be the student's aim. In the interests of objectivity no gesture, movement, sound or word should be rejected as of no interest or significance.

Themes for special study, after several studies of individual children, are innumerable. Locomotor, emotional, social, linguistic and intellectual aspects of development (themselves interrelated) each offer an enormous selection.

More complex designs for studies must not be confused with more complex themes or more elaborate methods. Observational techniques can be used within the more complex designs of:

cross-sectional studies
longitudinal studies
a combination of the two.

Before starting a more ambitious study of one of these kinds it is essential that a group of students, with proper tutorial guidance, make thoughtful decisions about how many children are to be observed, for what periods of time, within what total period, using which version of observational technique—and what each of the group understands by the words (e.g. 'quarrel', 'friendly overture', 'concentration') they are using in connexion with the study-theme.

There should be a progression throughout a training course from the close study of one child by one student, through small group-efforts at cross-sectional and then longitudinal studies, to larger group-undertakings of a combined cross-sectional and longitudinal investigation.

Professional research teams are becoming more likely every year to ask teachers, nursery assistants and other workers with children to help them in large-scale research. Experience such as that suggested in this book should be invaluable to anyone involved in such an enterprise.

6. Other Observational Techniques: Time-Sampling and Event-Sampling

In recording behaviour in the manner described in chapter 4 the observer records everything that happens—or at least as much of it as she can get down on paper—as it happens, and in a fairly substantial block of time, i.e. anything from five to fifteen or twenty minutes of continuous behaviour. She has, therefore, taken a specimen of a child's behaviour in much the same way as a geologist might obtain a core by drilling straight through one part of the earth's crust. The geologist with such a specimen can look at every layer in the sample, analyse the chemical constituents of each, notice how the banding lies, identify the fossils in each, and so on. Such an examination tells him a very great deal about the age, structure, sequence of events, composition and stresses of that particular part of the crust. What it cannot tell him is what the structure is like a mile away, ten miles away, or round the hill; it cannot tell him how and where the structure changes, or why. In order to discover these things he has to take small cores from drillings at predecided intervals across the landscape.

The student of child behaviour and development can do something very similar, and the technique she uses is called *time-sampling* of behaviour. At predecided intervals, say of fifteen or twenty minutes, a child is closely observed (exactly as in taking a specimen description) for one or two minutes only. Fifteen or twenty minutes later he is observed again, and again for only one minute or two minutes. Some investigators have used observation units of as little as ten seconds, but so short a period is not recommended for the novice. This sampling of behaviour goes on for perhaps every morning of a week, or for an afternoon period every other day, or for part of a day at weekly intervals, according to what time the student has available for child-study, and what it is hoped to detect.

Essential to good time-sampling are careful decisions, before the start of the study, about:

    i   the total length of time available—a week, several weeks, one day a week for a term, for example.

    ii   the size of the time-unit for close observation, one minute or two minutes probably being the most useful for a start.

    iii   the interval between units—fifteen, twenty or thirty minute intervals being sensible, hour intervals being suitable if there are to be several children studied over several months of a college term.

During the course of such sampling there might be temptations to go on recording beyond the minute or two minutes decided upon, if the child seems to be doing something very interesting. This temptation simply must be resisted. The object of the time-sampling technique is to get a picture of the child's typical rhythms of activity, rest, irritability and serenity, interests and social contact style, and this picture is badly blurred by uneven and 'loaded' sampling. If it is a particular type of behaviour that interests the observer, such as social overtures, creative work or language, time-sampling is not the best observational technique by which to study it. There are better and more efficient techniques by which to track and record a specific type of behaviour.

Time-sampling is a very good and efficient method indeed to find out what children do throughout a day, how they do it, and with whom, how long they tend to stay with one activity and what kind of person an individual is in total. It gives, in fact, an excellent picture of a child's typical responses across a fair length of time; and it reduces the risk of observing a really non-typical piece of behaviour for that particular child by taking only one specimen of twenty minutes on one day. The technique also allows, over a period of several weeks or even months, for a picture of progress—an important part of study of children. As a practical aid to learning by the student it is useful in that, as well as yielding the sort of information just listed, it allows her to study several children in one school, within the relatively limited time of a practice period, especially if she decides to use one-minute units of observation at twenty minute intervals.

The above description relates to time-sampling of total behaviour, i.e. the observer records everything the child does in the minute or two minutes during which he is being observed. There is a variation of time-sampling used by many investigators, however, which is useful to the student who has already had the essential experiences of specimen description and time-sampling of total behaviour. It is the use of the one or two minute unit of time in which to record only certain, predecided behaviours. The technique remains the same— the size of time-unit and interval, the exact recording method are as for time-sampling of total behaviour. The difference lies in the decision, carefully arrived at before observation takes place, of what to select and what to leave out of the record. Only that kind of behaviour which it is desired to study is recorded; anything else the child is doing in the minute or two minute period is not noted. The technique has been used to study social contacts, aggressive acts, solitary play, leadership, submissive behaviour, and a host of other such behaviours which reveal the 'grain' of personality.

It will be obvious that if some everyday social behaviour is studied there is likely to be something to record every minute that is sampled; with behaviours suspected to be less common there may be units of time in which there is nothing to record. In the latter case, it must be remembered that this 'nil return' is very important evidence—it shows how rarely something happens, which is essential to our understanding of children, and helps on occasions to explode myths about children in general or about a particular child. The writer once sampled, for one minute at fifteen minute intervals, over a period of five mornings, the 'bossy' behaviour of a lively and bombastic four year old, of whom the teacher said (exasperatedly), *He's ordering somebody about every five minutes—a proper little Hitler!* In fact, he 'bossed' other children only four times in the course of forty sampled units, and much more typical of his behaviour was the busy, talkative, co-operative play with other boys on trucks and on the climbing frame. He also had a surprising number of 'quiet' periods when he sat and told himself stories from books in the book-corner, or swung on a gate watching the groundsman at work. His 'bossiness' was illusory, to a great extent, and noted probably because when he did 'boss' other children he did it very loudly and with considerable effect! The same sort of exercise done with a little girl of 3 : 6, said to be clinging and over-dependent on adults, demonstrated that her teacher and nursery nurse were quite right—she was recorded as clinging, crying, wheedling or pressing close to the adult for over half the recorded unit of time, and was patently a very unhappy and disturbed child. There is always the danger, however, that a 'grizzling' child of one day, or short period of a day, who does tend to be a nuisance, if only temporarily, will be remembered by a busy adult as an over-demanding child in general, and a controlled study can be helpful in putting the record straight and avoiding 'labelling'.

If several students are co-operating in making this kind of selective time-sample of behaviour it is crucial to define terms before they start. What is going to count as 'clinging' or 'demanding' or 'aggressive' behaviour, to be recorded in those one or two minute units? There must always be discussion of terms, as has been said earlier in this book—for selective time-sampling the job is of such importance that the whole study can be a waste of time if agreement is not reached before the start. Every student could be recording, or not recording, something different unless each is sure that this or that behaviour exactly fits what they had defined as within their 'brief'.

Event-sampling is much more akin to bird-watching than are any of the other techniques so far described! It involves recording without having had prior warning of the event, and so having to be prepared with notebook at any time. It depends on what the child does at an unpredictable moment, not on the observer's previous decision to record all his behaviour, or a selected facet of it, at predecided intervals. It also demands that the student has more than average alertness to what is going on among a group of children, and must be prepared at any moment to leave what she is doing and record the kind of behaviour in which she is interested. For these reasons it is less useful to the student doing practice sessions in nursery or other school than it is to a mother, who is at home with one child and no duties to others at the time.

It is a valuable technique, however, for counting the number, intervals and duration of certain types of behaviour such as night-terrors or nightmares, tantrums, use of a certain piece of equipment or toy, solitary play (of children in school), quarrels or approaches to an adult. Every time the particular event occurs the observer notes time, place and circumstances, presence of other children etc., and then records the behaviour just as in taking a specimen description or a time-sample. The event may take one minute of time, or three, or ten—but it must be recorded in entirety and as full detail as possible. It may be found, by event sampling technique, that tantrums in a two year old almost always occur in the late afternoon; or that a four year old's solitary play takes place, almost always, after the midday meal; or that a six year old plays with his 'dinky' cars much less often than had been supposed; or that nightmares occur most frequently when father is away from home. (These are hypothetical cases, given only as examples of the kind of information that can be gained from the technique; they are certainly not 'norms' of behaviour, and must not be quoted as such.)

It is most important that the basic technique of specimen description be practised before others are tried—and that it should be used at intervals with children being studied by means of the other observational techniques to give a 'depth' picture of a child. The obvious drawback to time-sampling and event-sampling is that much behaviour is not recorded. For the person who has had several, or many, years of experience with children this may not matter very much. For the novice, however, it is essential to her understanding that she go back, over and over again, to the specimen description, if only to take one or two fifteen minute samples every term. If she uses only the time-sampling technique, and particularly the selective version of it, she may well end up with a fragmentary and somewhat 'lop-sided' view of how children at different ages behave. Ideally, the student should be helped to expertise in all these observational techniques, and to use of those which are most appropriate to each task. Event-sampling has particular snags for the novice, who may well decide that she is interested in one aspect of children's behaviour and record only that, failing to relate this one aspect to any of the rest of the behaviour, and thus remaining unable to see its significance in the whole life of the child.

It is strongly recommended that event-sampling be left until some considerable experience of children, and of child-study has been gained.

There is a kind of study, using observational techniques of either specimen description or time-sampling (preferably employing both, in turn), which involves students, singly or in small groups, observing not a specific child or children but a specific piece of apparatus or equipment—the water-tank, the sandpit, the painting area or the climbing frame, for example, in a nursery or Infants' school; the mathematics area, or the library corner, might be suitable provision to observe when dealing with older children. It is often claimed that children 'enjoy' certain activities more than they do others, or that 'they hardly ever use the book-corner', or that this or that provision is over- or under-used. It is a most interesting exercise to test such claims, beliefs and preferences—and, in addition, to note which children use the materials or equipment being observed, how often, for how long, and in what manner. Have the girls a virtual monopoly of the house-corner, or do boys come there as often? Does each child who comes stay as long? Use the same equipment in the 'house'? Play out similar roles? Or are there differences by sex, age, home backgrounds or even time of day? Is water used for the same purposes by three year olds, six year olds or children in a junior school? Does play in the sandpit tend to be solitary, co-operative or comfortably 'communal'? Is it always concerned with construction? Or do imaginative games take place there? A great deal has yet to be learned about the use children make of what we adults take to be good provision. No student who has made several such studies in her training years is likely to fall into the error of supposing that because we have traditionally supposed certain materials and certain equipment to be 'good' for children they will use it, enjoy it equally, or make the sort of use of it that we have expected. The controlled study of children's use of provision is a relatively simple but enormously interesting and revealing exercise.

Summary

Time-sampling involves observing a child closely for one or two minutes every fifteen, twenty, or thirty minutes, over a reasonably long period of time—as, every morning for a week, or on each afternoon, or for one session a week over a term—and recording his total behaviour.

It gives a picture of his characteristic rhythms of activity and his general interests. To get an accurate picture the recording must be confined to the predecided time-unit, and not allowed to 'run on'.

Selective time-sampling involves using the same time-units and intervals, and the same accurate recording, but only of a predecided type of behaviour. If none of this is taking place in the period of observation the 'nil return' is as important as a positive recording.

Event-sampling is the recording, whenever and wherever it takes place, of certain behaviours that are of particular interest to the observer, e.g. nightmares, tantrums, solitary play, approaches to adults. It is a very useful technique for a mother; not so useful to the student who has to look after a group of children and may not be able to leave them at a second's notice to record the 'event'.

It is a useful technique by which to test number, duration and circumstances surrounding certain behaviours that puzzle or worry teachers or parents.

Return to the specimen description should be made at intervals, when children are being studied by time-sampling or event-sampling techniques, in order that a 'depth' picture of an individual child be built up.

Observation not of a single child or selected group of children but of a piece of equipment (e.g. water-tank, house-corner, sandpit) with a view to finding out how many children use it, how often, and for what purposes is a most valuable exercise, and strongly recommended.

7. Sorting Out the Data

Throughout the course students will have been finding their way about the literature of child development and (unless they are very advanced and experienced people indeed) most of the literature they will use is of the textbook variety. There are, however, excellent journals of the learned kind that are by no means beyond the understanding of the novice, providing she is offered some guidance in tracing them, and in interpreting their reports. This is often, in fact, a most rewarding group exercise, under the guidance of a tutor. For the purposes of this book, however, it is probably sensible to refer only to textbooks which are reasonably easy for students to obtain either by purchase or from college libraries.

Most students will realize that the child development books fall into broad categories, although with inevitable overlap, of the following kinds:

  i Descriptive texts, dealing with development generally (e.g. Gabriel, 1968)
 ii Books almost entirely concerned with graded scales of performance (e.g. Griffiths, 1954; Gesell, 1954)
iii Works on one aspect of development only (e.g. Wilkinson, 1972, on language)
 iv Large reference works, containing papers, or chapters, by many experts and covering all aspects of development (e.g. Carmichael, 1963, 2nd ed.)
  v Large reference works, also by many contributors, containing chapters on different aspects of one part

of development (e.g. Mussen, Conger and Kagan, 1969, on personality)

vi Books containing incidental reference to developmental matters, but mainly concerned with social conditions and influences (e.g. Butler, Davie and Goldstein, 1972)

Obviously, books such as Van der Eyken's *The Preschool Years* and Winnicott's *The Child, the Family and the Outside World* can be read straight through even by the beginner, and contain valuable insights. They set the scene, and help students to develop concepts of childhood. Others cannot be read in this way, and were not intended for such use. They are for reference, and students should learn early to use contents pages and index to find specific chapters or passages for their own purposes. It is pointless, for example, to begin at page one of Gesell's *The First Five Years of Life* and read through to the end. No one could possibly remember that much material, and very dull the task would be even if one could. The same is true of Gabriel's, admittedly more readable, *Children Growing Up*. If the child being studied is a two year old, Gesell's and Gabriel's sections on that age-group will be all that is needed from those two texts. Thereafter, it is advisable to look up what Griffiths has to say about the age-group in *The Abilities of Babies*, and add to the already growing store of information what Sheridan's norms can offer. If it is possible to see the Robertson's film *A Two Year Old Goes to Hospital* the extent of the student's knowledge will be even greater, and her understanding greatly extended. She can add to her store, perhaps, by tracking down references in Carmichael, and reading relevant passages on language in Wilkinson. It is up to the individual student, in fact, to gather as much information as she can, from as many sources as she can lay her hands on, about the age-group to which 'her' child belongs. At no stage should she feel that to read one book on two year olds is enough—even if she could find so limited and limiting a volume.

What the wise student is doing is building up a picture of what is involved in being two years old; and while she is doing this from good 'second hand' sources (i.e. the textbooks) she is actively involved with a real two year old, whom she is closely observing. The over-particular view one gets of child-hood from knowing one child well is extended by the reading; the theoretical and sometimes stylized view of childhood one can get from reading alone is corrected by the antics and affection of the live child. In any case, the study of real children should always precede reading about them, if only by a matter of days or a week or two. It is fatally easy to read something for the first time about (say) a two year old, and be so interested in it, even excited by the knowledge, that one tends to 'see' it in some behaviour of the first two year old studied—even though what he is doing is not really what the book described at all. Look first; read soon afterwards; go back to the child; and read some more. This is the best way to avoid the pitfalls of over-partisanship, over-theorizing, and seeing what is not really there.

ii

In pursuing this combination of looking, recording and read-ing, it will become apparent that what is called the 'raw data', i.e. the student's own observations of on-going behaviour, has to be analysed in some way. Otherwise it remains a sort of interesting heap of treasure but has little use in discussion, consideration of developmental characteristics of specific kinds, essay writing or relation to children studied later. The first task, when faced with the notebook full of specimen descriptions or time-samples, is to sort it out into broad cate-gories of child behaviour. In real life, and as he goes about his everyday pursuits, a child does not involve himself in 'language development' for one period, move on to 'social development' and then concentrate on his 'locomotor develop-ment'. In all his activities he is developing all his abilities at once—words accompanying movement, both often involving social interaction, the whole activity feeding curiosity and therefore 'intellectual' development. Everything being said, done and thought brings the child into greater exploration of materials, tools and his own confidence in using them. Nevertheless, if some sorting out of individual aspects of development is not done the student is left uncertain of just how many things are happening at once, and what is the importance of each. So long as we do not forget that such sorting out into separate categories of behaviour is just a device for our own better learning, and remember always that each child grows as a totally integrated whole person, the analysing of what he does into separate categories is useful.

Most often, it is recommended that students accept the categories used by the distinguished investigators of child behaviour. Although these are called by slightly different names by different writers, they cover, in each set of norms or scales, the same set of behaviours:

Locomotor and hand-and-eye
Social-emotional
Language
Intellectual

The kinds of behaviour that can be listed under each of these has already been suggested at the beginning of Chapter 5. Students will soon realize that what Gesell refers to as gross and fine locomotor skills Griffiths sorts into two separate categories as locomotor and eye-hand; that what Gesell calls adaptive behaviour Griffiths lists under 'performance'; that the 'language' category of Gesell is the 'hearing and speech' category of Griffiths. It does not matter which writer's list of names is used (Sheridan's are very slightly different again) so long as the student is clear as to which she is using, and what kinds of behaviour she is going to sort into each category.

Language is easy to identify. It should all be recorded in the right-hand margin, or column, of the notebook, and separated during actual recording from the other activities. But it is important to scrutinize the main column of the record to find out if there is evidence that a child understood something said to him, even if he did not utter sound or word in response. The understanding a child has of what others say is just as important a part of his language development as his own spoken word (or babbled sound). This, by the way, is where the items and category of Griffiths are more helpful than the general label 'language' used by Gesell. Griffiths, by including the word 'hearing' in her category-label, underlines the importance of noticing what a child has heard and acted upon, even without making vocal response to it. All babies, and indeed all people, have a far greater understanding vocabulary than they have a spoken one. A word of warning may be in place here, however—the obliging way in which children will listen to adults explaining, or reproving, or telling them a story sometimes leads adults to think that a child has understood every word and really 'got the drift' of the explanation, reproof or story when he may have done nothing of the kind. While acknowledging that every child understands much more than he actually expresses in words, it is also true that there is much in adult language, and even the language of an older but still young child that he misunderstands or that simply 'goes over his head'.

Locomotor behaviour, whether concerned with large or fine movements (the eye-hand category of Griffiths), is also reasonably easy to identify. There is, after all, no doubt that a description of a child climbing the stairs, or riding his tricycle, or throwing a ball is to be listed as 'locomotor'. Similarly, holding a pencil, picking beads out of a box, cutting with scissors, placing one block on another, and such activities obviously involve fine locomotor, or eye-and-hand abilities.

Social behaviour is easily identified, since it involves the child's interaction with another person or persons, and will be clearly identified in the record by the presence of square brackets round the behaviour and/or language of the other person. However, there is sometimes a little puzzlement as to whether seemingly sociable play is actually social at all—as when a group of two year olds play alongside each other in a sandpit, tolerating each other, and perhaps even seeming to enjoy the presence of others, but never exchanging a word or sharing a tool or looking at each other's efforts. This is a matter for careful scrutiny of the record, for discussion with tutor or fellow-students, and for a look in one or two textbooks, before deciding whether such behaviour is to be categorized as 'social' or as (perhaps) only eye-and-hand, or eye-and-hand and performance.

Performance (*Griffiths*) or *Adaptive Behaviour* (*Gesell*) are more difficult categories to sort out. What is meant by these labels is the use children make of materials; what they actually do with the equipment they use; how, in fact, they adapt the toys, tools, materials and equipment of their world to uses of their own. A baby putting a spoon in and out of a cup, and rattling it, repeating the performance with head cocked on one side as though listening, and repeating the action over and over again, has obviously adapted the 'tools' to pleasurable and experimental uses of his own. He is 'performing' an act initiated by himself. A four year old building with blocks or waste materials, a seven year old designing a motor-way system with blocks, card, sand and oddments all over the floor is also to be categorized as indulging in highly adaptive behaviour, or (if using Griffiths' term) displaying a high level of performance with materials.

It is obvious that adaptive behaviour, or performance, must include other abilities—gross locomotor, fine locomotor and often language as well. Such activities, therefore, are usually listed under several categories.

When the record has been studied in a general way, and the sorts of behaviours to be categorized understood, it is necessary to find some manner in which to identify them at a glance on the record sheets. The writer's advice to students has always been to use coloured pencils, ball-point pens or felt pens; to decide on a colour for each of the categories (apart from language, which is already separated, in any case); and to go through the record underlining (for example) every locomotor incident in red, every social item in green, and so on. (Out of consideration for a tutor who may have to glance over some twenty or thirty records it is also advisable for a group of students to agree, with the tutor, on a common code —so that in every student's record every underlining in red is of a locomotor item, every blue line is indicating adaptive behaviour etc.) Once this is done it is often surprising to realize how much a child's behaviour over the total time in which his behaviour was sampled 'clusters' under one particular category. It is also interesting and important to note that a child's behaviour has a different emphasis in different periods over (say) a three-month period of time. One observation of a nineteen-month-old child, for example, may show almost nothing in the language column during one series of observations; a fortnight later the records of that same child may show so much babble, jargon and real words that the column is hardly large enough to contain it. Such emphases and 'spurts' show up almost at a glance as the coloured underlinings are completed.

Another useful device is to draw a line in black round each unit of behaviour. For example, if the first five minutes of a record, containing items of locomotor, social, language and eye-and-hand aspects, takes place with one set of materials in one part of the room with mother being part of the child's 'scene', this constitutes a recognizable unit or module of activity; the next five or six minutes might involve another sort of play in the hallway, with another sort of toy or material, and another person being involved—or no other person at all—and this is obviously another unit or module. To note such modules of behaviour, recorded carefully in time, is to get a good idea of the child's concentration period, degree of persistence, main interests and mobility.

iii

Having underlined different activities in colour throughout the record and drawn 'blocks' round modules of behaviour, the student is in a position to put some of the data into a neater and more readable form than that on her rapidly scribbled, and now garishly coloured and scored sheets. She can, for instance, plot the proportions of time spent in various kinds of activity by the child. This can be done only approximately, by counting the number of underlined items, but it can give a useful and 'telling' profile of the child's activity during periods of observation. The following is the kind of simplified record that can be extracted from the rough, original notebook:

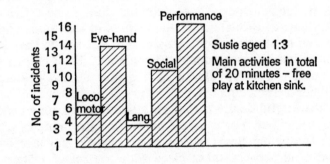

This is how one child of fifteen months spent twenty minutes of her time, with mother present, and playing with bottles, spoons, cups, two stoppers, a sink-tidy and cloth in a sink filled with clean water. It is apparent from the histogram above that she was dexterous (a lot of eye-hand items noted), absorbed with her skills (twenty minutes is a long period for a child to concentrate at this age), made some social overtures (waves and smiles at her mother), and had no need in this particular period for large movement. Nevertheless, her sure posture on the chair as she stood at the sink, her confident reaching for the taps and for articles on the draining board, and her ease in turning round suggested good locomotor ability; it was in observations made later, in the garden, that a high number of locomotor items were noted, in fact.

At exactly the same age, but in the situation of many playthings and presence of older siblings, the following 'picture' was made of another child, and demonstrates how variable is the emphasis on various aspects of development according to child, situation and presence of others:

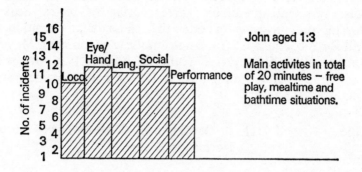

John aged 1:3

Main activites in total of 20 minutes — free play, mealtime and bathtime situations.

Another means of recording relative emphasis on different aspects of development is by means of the pie-graph, as under:

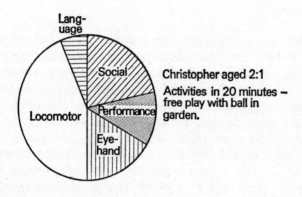

Christopher aged 2:1

Activities in 20 minutes — free play with ball in garden.

In addition to these first and approximate pictures of how 'her' child spends his time, and develops his abilities and skills, it is important for the student to have some idea of how the one child she has now studied closely compares with others of his age. It is here that the normative scales are useful (i.e. after, rather than before, making first-hand observations). There are simple ways of recording such comparisons, and many tutors will have excellent suggestions of their own. One way, however, is to make a table such as that below, using at least two, and preferably three, normative scales. Scales developed by investigators other than those already mentioned will be recommended by some tutors (e.g. those of M. M. Shirley, 1933; Bayley, 1933; and C. Bühler, 1935, are still valid and useful scales) and it hardly matters which are employed, for a start.

Giles   Aged 1:11   Development Compared with Three Normative Scales

Aspect	Giles	Griffiths	Sheridan	Gesell	Comments on Giles
Locomotor	Runs, slight swerve. Climbs	Item no....	Item no...	Item no...	Typical behaviour
Eye-hand	Screws large knobs. Holds brush well	Item no...	Item no...	Item no...	Possibly a little advanced
Language ↑ etc					Very slightly below norm

Where there are discrepancies between scales (and there are bound to be a few slight ones, when one considers the different countries of origin and periods at which the scales were standardized), there must be thoughtful group discussion of why these might exist in relation to a particular item. Where there are discrepancies between the behaviour of the child studied and the norm of one or more scales, these, too, should be calmly accepted and discussed with informed interest. It must always be remembered that no child will conform exactly to every norm in every aspect, for individuality is unmeasurable. Indeed, a chart showing that a particular child conformed to every norm would be a most highly suspect piece of work!

iv

Comparing her own findings with those of other members of her group, each of whom has probably studied a child of a different age, is the next and essential part of the analytic job. After the individual histograms or pie-graphs, tabulations and comparisons with normative scales have been made, group members should have organized discussion with each other, and build up some kind of summary of development, at least to cover one or two aspects of development, if not all.

One way of doing this is to sketch a table on a large blackboard, with appropriate headings, and get each student to call out what 'her' child did in that aspect—encouraging each contributor to be brief and clear (e.g. saying 'Climbs stairs on hands and knees', and not giving a whole sketch of the child's behaviour!) The recorder by the board has to be able to write quickly and neatly—tutors are usually the most experienced people to do this—and build up a picture of development before the eyes of the group, which, of course, is fully participant. The resultant chart, for locomotor development, in this case, would look something like this at the end of the session:

Locomotor Development from 3m. to 2y. 3m. using: Students' Studies of Twenty Children

Name	Age	Large movement	Fine movement	Remarks
Simon	3m			A very active child
Amanda	7m	Brief description	of activities	Slow, gentle child
Caroline	10m	noted entered	in these columns	Lively, but just recovered from a cold
Jeremy	12m			Slight eye defect
Peter	14m			Large, heavy child
etc.				etc.

The larger the student group the more tedious such an exercise can become, and it is recommended that after an initial demonstration large groups be broken down into smaller ones to continue their tabulations on their own.

Further, it is probably not necessary to make a chart to cover each aspect of development, but to let smaller groups make charts for language, or social behaviour, or one aspect that interests them, and to display them for others to see in the tutorial or lecture room.

b. A large grid can be drawn on paper, and each student asked to fill in items from her own study under the appropriate headings. The chart can then be used as a basis for discussion of several selected aspects.

c. Items from one or more normative scales can be listed down one side of a large sheet, and students asked to insert examples of 'their' children's performance in this particular alongside.

d. A group of students can be divided into small working-parties and each asked to produce a display of charts (using one or several of the above forms), graphs, histograms etc., a paper on some aspect of interest to be read to the group, and a list of references relevant to the material presented.

In any of the above exercises what is being used throughout as a basis are original observations made by students themselves. All the quite dramatic demonstrations of development in the first five or six years of life that will be produced in tabulations, graphs and written material will have been derived not from textbooks, in the first instance, but from observations of real children, each one of whom is known to at least one student in the group. The references to work read are passed on to fellow students, to form a useful bibliography, and are absolutely relevant because fellow-students found them so. Short papers read to the group will have immediacy and interest, because findings will have been original and the work of students themselves.

The 'block' lecture; private reading without specific purpose; lack of outlet and real use for painstakingly gathered data; and the artificiality and isolation of essay-writing on somebody else's choice of theme—all are avoided by some version of the analytic approach to child-study sketched above. From the start of their courses students start not only to use their own eyes and seek out relevant texts for themselves, but to work together as research teams, in however modest a manner, and produce their own learning material from the children they have studied with such care. There will be a tendency to use textbooks to extend personal experience, rather than to replace it, a live interest in sharing experience rather than grim determination to amass somebody else's facts about children unknown.

Relevance and commitment can be restored to learning through the medium of good child-study, in a manner that may not have been felt by many students since they themselves left the Infants' school. There is, in fact, no other area of study so important to the whole human race as the study of its children. There is no other area of which any one of us can say *I once knew this in my own life and in my own body and mind*. Because we were all children, all of us can become good students of child behaviour; the theme is never irrelevant or artificial unless teachers make it so.

As experience is gained, and the novice becomes a skilled observer, she will develop other means of observation, learn to use the tests and measures of psychology, perhaps, and devise more exact and sophisticated methods of analysing her data. But she should return, over and over again, to the close watching of children themselves, and the analysis of on-going behaviour which was recorded as it happened. Over the years of her course she should build up a personal file of sound observations, careful analyses, summaries of group projects, and relevant references—all covering children from birth to, say, the sixth or seventh years of life. Each unit within a file might thus consist of:

    a. a sample of first-hand observations
    b. histograms and other graphic presentation
    c. comparison of child behaviour observed with that on normative scales
    d. notes on team-work undertaken
    e. a brief summary, perhaps in short essay form, of the individual child studied
    f. a bibliography, including specific chapter or even page references, relevant to the child studied.

A set of these units of work constitutes the foundations on which not only future, and more sophisticated child-study will be built, but the source book for understanding of the children each novice will one day, as the experienced teacher or nursery nurse or child-care worker, have in her charge.

Summary
It is important to discriminate between different kinds of child-development literature, and to make proper use of each kind.
As many texts as possible should be consulted after study of one child of a particular age, in order to build up a detailed picture of how others have viewed children of this age.
Simple underlining, using a colour code, should be used to pick out activities of certain (predecided) kinds in the rough observation notebook.
Lines should be drawn round recognizable units (or modules) of activity.
Some simple graphic form should be used to illustrate relative concentration on certain aspects of development.
Comparison of the behaviour of the child studied with that of items in normative scales should be made in some simple tabulated form; more than one set of norms should be used.
Discrepancies, between the behaviour of the child studied and the norms, and between norms of different scales, should be discussed.
Comparison of one student's study with those of the rest of the group should be made next, as whole-group or small-group exercises. Four ways in which this might be done are suggested—but others may suggest themselves, and more than one sort of comparative exercise should be undertaken.
All the work based on first-hand child studies has the merit of immediacy and relevance, giving meaning to texts and practice in working as a team.
The result of a good course in child study is a record, at depth and in detail, of several children observed closely, and well recorded data on many more children studied by fellow students.

Kinds of Sample derived from Different Observational Techniques

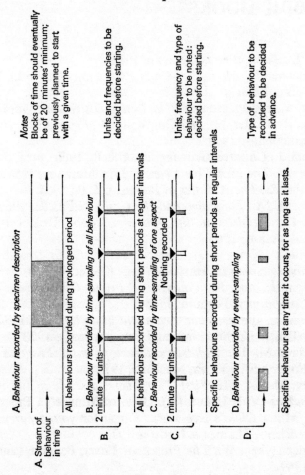

The above diagram is a graphic summary of what is described in Chapters 5 and 6. Choice of observational technique will depend on what kind of information is being sought—but the specimen description technique should always be used and thoroughly mastered before attempts are made at other approaches.

Useful Books

Berg, L., *Look at Kids*, Penguin, 1972

Carmichael, L., *Manual of Child Psychology* (2nd ed.), Wiley, N.Y., 1963.

Clegg, A., and Megson, B., *Children in Distress*, Penguin, 1970

Davie, R., Butler, N., and Goldstein, H., *From Birth to Seven*, Longmans, 1972

Gabriel. J., *Children Growing Up*, U.L.P., 1968

Gesell, A., *The First Five Years of Life*, Methuen, 1954

Griffiths, R., *The Abilities of Babies*, U.L.P., 1954

Lewis, M. M., *Language and the Child*, N.F.E.R., 1969

May, D., *Children in the Nursery School*, Bristol Inst. of Education, 1963

Mussen, P., Conger, J., and Kagan, J., *Child Development and Personality*, Harper & Row (3rd ed.), 1969

Newson, J., and E., *Patterns of Infant Care in an Urban Community*, Penguin, 1965

Newson, J., and E., *Four Years Old in an Urban Community*, Allen & Unwin, 1968, and Penguin (n.e.), 1970

Sheridan, M. D., *Children's Developmental Progress from Birth to Five Years*, N.F.E.R., 1973

Shirley, M. M., *The First Two Years: a study of twenty-five babies* (Vols II and III), Univ. of Minnesota Press, 1933

Sime, M., *A Child's Eye View: Piaget for young parents and teachers*, Thames & Hudson, 1973

Van der Eyken, W., *The Preschool Years*, Penguin (2nd ed.), 1969

Webb, L., *Modern Practice in the Infant School*, Blackwell, 1969

Wilkinson, A. M., *The Foundations of Language*, O.U.P., 1971

Winnicott, D. W., *The Child, the Family and the Outside World*, Penguin, 1964